Just Give Me God

by

Nathan L. Simmons

Vincom Publishing Co.
Tulsa, Oklahoma

Unless otherwise indicated, all Scripture quotations are taken from the *King James Version* of the Bible.

All Scripture quotations marked NIV are taken from *The Holy Bible, New International Version*. Copyright © 1973, 1978, 1984 by The International Bible Society. Used by permission of Zondervan Bible Publishers.

Just Give Me God
ISBN 0-927936-51-8

1517 Ralph David Abernathy Boulevard
Atlanta, Georgia 30310

Published by
VINCOM PUBLISHING CO.
P. O. Box 702400
Tulsa, Oklahoma 74170
(918) 254-1276

Printed in the United States of America.

Acknowledgments

Special thanks to Presiding Bishop Gilbert Earl Patterson, Bishop Charles Blake, and Bishop Chandler D. Owens.

To the faithful members of the Citadel of Hope International Church of God in Christ, thank you for releasing me to the Body of Christ and allowing me the time to produce this project.

To Evangelist Donna Marie Jones, thank you for your endurance, patience, encouragement, and fine-tuning. What would I do without you?

Thank you, Brother Wayne Williams! You are God-sent and I appreciate your God-given talents.

Thank you to George Vinnett and Vincom Publishing Company. You are invaluable!

To my wife Angelic and my beautiful daughters, Victoria and Alexis, thank you for your love and tender care.

Contents

Introduction:

New Dimensions, Not New Levels

Often we hear Christians say, "I want to go to another level in God," and in fact, I even prayed that myself. "Oh, Lord, in this meeting, I want to take the saints to a new level in You."

Suddenly the Holy Spirit quickened my spirit like a bolt of lightning and said, "Nathan, I do not want to take the saints to *another level*. Another level just means they can be the same people doing the same things with the same people, wearing the same clothing, having the same mentality — the same attitudes, dispositions, and outlooks."

I finally understand that He meant the devil can find you at another level, *because you are yet at the same place*. The things still in your life of the soul or flesh that hinder you will surface again in different ways at different levels.

Old-fashioned sanctification meant praying through to a different place in God, one where old things had passed away.

In this new century, the Church must move into new territory and new arenas, or we will not accomplish God's will for this generation. I know from my travels to different congregations that many Christians are tired of the "same old same old."

They have exhausted all their resources, tried everything they know in spiritual things, and find themselves in the same rut. They are still having to deal with the same old problems: pride, fear, discouragement, finances, marriage and parental problems.

The Body of Christ is in an awesome time, a time when we have tried everything from natural programs to operating in the supernatural. This may sound discouraging, and a lot of Christians *are* discouraged, and some have fallen away. Others have resigned themselves to living in less than victory and even apathy.

Some are complacent, thinking they are okay on their present level when they actually are still babes in Christ. These are the "lukewarm" ones spoken of in the book of The Revelation of Jesus Christ to the Apostle John. (Revelation 3:16.)

However, the Church really is in a good place: a place of coming to the end of our own resources and being forced to believe that God is able to do "exceeding abundantly" above all we could ever imagine. (Ephesians 3:20.) There is an old saying that contains all the truth we need for the present time: *Just let go and let God.*

When you are at the end of yourself and cry wholeheartedly, *"Just give me God,"* you are finally in a place where God can change you and change the things that pertain to your life. As long as you are trying to "do it yourself," even on a different level, He will let you.

When you come to the end of yourself and turn everything over to Him — lay everything on the altar, including self — there is hope. You will then be at an entirely different place in God.

God has moved His Church to a place where we must depend totally on Him. Whatever we depended on in the 90s cannot be depended on now for certain. Crops fail, disasters strike, the economy is shaky with the job situation insecure, and fuel and food prices are going higher. However, we can have optimism *if* we only depend on God as our Source: spirit, soul, and body.

Looking at Church history, we can see that over and over God brought His people full circle to a place where they understand that it is only **in him we live, and move, and have our being** (Acts 17:28).

Unfortunately, it seems that Christians and the Church en masse do not depend solely on God in prosperous times. It takes the "rug being pulled out from under us" to cause many of us to cast everything over on God.

I do not know what the hard thing is in your life. I do not know the exact circumstances or situations or problems with which you are dealing. I do know this: **There is no new thing under the sun** (Ecclesiastes 1:9).

Regardless of your education, your financial situation, your family background or where you live, your problems are not new.

Regardless of your profession or your situation in life, from rich man to poor, minister to maintenance man, man to woman, there is nothing with which you are struggling that is unique.

Also, there is one answer to all of it: God.

If God cannot do it, it cannot be done.

If God cannot do it, you certainly cannot, nor can the government, the law, or society.

I pray the truths in this book will help you to understand that *now is the time to ask God*. Regardless of whether it is sickness, financial problems, spiritual problems, job or career problems, marital or child problems, even mental or emotional problems, the answer is God. Whether I am facing success or failure at the moment, I am to seek God.

If you think you have prayed and asked God but nothing is happening, perhaps you have not asked the right thing.

Perhaps you have not completely turned everything over to Him.

Perhaps you have things in your own life that are hindering His answer. Keep asking, seeking, and knocking.

Perhaps it is the enemy holding up your answer as he once did for the prophet Daniel. (Daniel 10:13), in which case, you need to fast and pray or just keep holding on in faith for your answer.

The bottom line is that it is time for us, individually and corporately, to *ask God for a hard thing*, whatever that may be.

There are examples throughout Scripture of this, but one man I want to "hone in" on in particular is Elisha. We need to understand what was going on when he asked God for a hard thing through his mentor, Elijah, and what happened when he got it.

1

Ask God for a Hard Thing: Dare to Ask for More

. . . Thou hast asked a *hard thing*: nevertheless, if thou see me when I am taken from thee, it shall be so unto thee; but if not, it shall not be so.

2 Kings 2:10

To understand this concept, we must go beyond Saturn, Mars, and Jupiter, beyond the stars and moon, but we are truly going back to the future, back to almost 900 years before Christ — and yet, to a time in our own future *if* we learn from Elisha. Dare to ask for more.

Let me set the scene for when these two exceptional men of God, Elijah and Elisha, lived and served God so mightily. They had no books of the Bible named after them. Yet they were mighty men of God, who had major effects on the history of God's people, and who did mighty deeds.

When Jesus began His ministry, two of the things He did reflected the models of these two men. Jesus' actions made a statement to those of the Jewish people, the remnant of the Israelites, who had spiritual discernment. His "acting out" the pattern of Elijah and Elisha plainly told those with ears to hear and eyes to see (Matthew 13:9) that He was Messiah.

1. Jesus fulfilled 40 days and nights of fasting in the desert as had Elijah, who was considered a model of the ideal prophet, yet only a forerunner of Messiah. (1 Kings 19:8; Matthew 4:2.)

2. Jesus' miracle of the loaves and fishes (Matthew 16:9,10) fulfilled Elisha's miracle of feeding 100 men with 20 loaves. (2 Kings 4:42.)

We do not understand how the leaders of Judea could see these things acted out in front of them and still doubt Jesus' divinity. However, the reason is that their traditions — and the religion that had grown up around them — had replaced Scripture, had become a "veil" upon their heart. (2 Corinthians 3:15.).)

Paul wrote that this "veil" has been done away with in Christ. (2 Corinthians 3:14.) Yet we can be guilty of the same blindness if we let the traditions of religion blind us to the real moving of Jesus in our day.

They were praying in Jesus' day for Messiah to deliver them from Rome. They were praying for a *hard thing*. However, they were praying for a wrong hard thing, so they missed God altogether.

Be sure that you are praying rightly when you pray for a hard thing. Do not dictate to God what that is, how it will come, or when it will come, or you may not see Him when He passes by with your answer.

The reports of Elijah and Elisha in 1 and 2 Kings show that neither came from the ruling class. In fact, Elijah's background is left a mystery. He just suddenly walked into the pages of history, a man full of righteous indignation and sent by God to direct His people back to right paths.

Your father does not have to be wealthy or a bishop, and your mother does not have to be a teacher or a leader of the church ladies' group for God to use you. God can pull you out of addictions, a life of crime, or even the street scene, *if you answer His call*.

I believe there are many spiritual Elishas in the Church today all over the world, because this is one of those pivotal times in history. This is a time when God's people are being called to new places in Him, not just new levels of the same place.

Elijah and Elisha had to accept God's call and move into new places in their lives, places of total commitment to God, places of being willing to die if that became necessary, places where the supernatural is more real than the natural, and places where fear of man does not exist.

At one point in Elijah's life, he did succumb to fear, fear of Jezebel, queen of Israel. However, when God called him to new assignments, he came out of the wilderness of discouragement and obeyed. (1 Kings 19:19.)

When you go to new places in God, sometimes you can become afraid of the strange and unique developments in this new territory. Sometimes you can become curious about what God is trying to accustom you to and feel as if you are stepping out on nothing. Because the new place is so alien to your old ways and thoughts, it feels as if you are swimming upstream against the current — and you are.

The farther upstream toward God that you go, the more pressure comes against you. However, if you "hang in there," soon you will realize that you are not "stepping out on nothing" but standing on a "Solid Rock," Jesus. You will realize that He has fought the upstream current already.

He has made a way for you to move upward in peace and quiet in the middle of riptides. In Him, you cannot be swept out to sea and lost as long as you have no tolerance for the things of the world that are trying to sweep you the other way.

Two Zero-Tolerance Men

Elijah and Elisha stood "flat-footed" and firm on the ways of God, on God's sovereignty, and in God's anointing and power. They had no tolerance for the pagan ways that had crept into Israel or the compromising that had crept into Judah. They were focused.

We might call these great men the elder and the younger. Elijah's name means *My God Is Jehovah.*[1] He has been called "the grandest and most romantic character" the Israelites ever produced. His successor, Elisha or the younger prophet, is named *God Is Salvation.*[2]

Names were not labels in ancient times, but words that carried literal meanings. Each time a person spoke to either of these men, they were speaking truths.

They were saying, "Hello, there, My-God-is-Jehovah," or "How do you do, God-is-salvation."

In the Greek transliteration, the elder's name is *Elias*, which means "God stands up" in this man.

If there is anyone I want to stand up in me it is God!

"Oh, God," I pray, "when I least expect You to stand up in me, give me holy boldness. Enable me to speak of You to men in every walk of life.

"Stand up in me so that I can cry aloud on street corners, with a platform that causes all to hear from Your mouth and Your heart, sparing none. Stand up in me so that I can go into crack houses and places where no one else wants to go and proclaim that My-God-is-Jehovah and You-are-salvation."

I love studying and preaching about the elder and the younger prophets because their personalities never get in the way of our seeing what God is doing through them. Their backgrounds and cultures never get in the way of God.

In their time, the people of Israel had divided into two kingdoms: Israel in the north and Judah in the south. Both nations were populated by Israelites descended from Abraham through Isaac, Jacob, and his 12 sons.

The united kingdom only lasted about 120 years under its first three kings: Saul, David, and Solomon. At the time of Elijah and

Elisha, God's people were two nations that sometimes lived next to each other in peace and sometimes were at war.

Israel with its capital of Samaria was populated mostly by particularly stiff-necked, hardheaded, and rebellious Israelites. They refused David as king for seven years and six months (2 Samuel 2:11), then broke away completely under Solomon's son, Rehoboam.

At the time of Elijah's sudden appearance, Israel's king, Ahab, had married a high priestess of a pagan, satanic cult from the neighboring nation of Sidon. His 22-year reign marked the depths of spiritual decline in the nation of the northern ten and a half tribes.

Jezebel was the "power behind the throne." She and her hundreds of priests almost crowded out the people of God. It was a time when it looked as if the enemy had won. American society today is called "post-Christian." The society in Israel in Elijah's day could have been called "post-Mosaic" or "post-Jehovah."

Then, if you read the book of 1 Kings, you know what happened. Some 7000 people in the nation who had not bowed their knees to Baal (1 Kings 19:18) must have gotten to the end of themselves and *asked God for a hard thing*.

God sent Elijah to give Israel what really amounted to her last chance to remain a nation, but the lessons learned then did not last, unfortunately. Less than 200 years later, the ten and a half tribes of Israelites making up the kingdom of Israel were taken into slavery by Assyria and disappeared from history. (1 Chronicles 5:26.)

Judah, the southern kingdom of two and one-half tribes, continued as a nation for several centuries longer (from 720 B.C. to 580 B.C.), and their descendants have remained visible down through history.

Judah remained closer to God and the teachings of the fathers from the prophet Samuel to Isaiah and the minor prophets. Three mysteries seem to be shown through Judah: the mystery of the continuing existence of the Israelites whom we now call the Jewish people, the mystery of God, and the contrasting mystery of iniquity.

Three Mysteries

Israel/Judah were the only people since Noah who walked in the mysteries of God until Jesus came and ushered in the Kingdom on earth. This Kingdom is the one whose citizens are all those born again of whatever gender, race, social class, or nationality. (Galatians 3:28,29.) We might call this *the mystery of the kingdom*, or the mystery of God's covenants with mankind.

The grace, mercy, and love of God, as well as His peace, passes all of man's understanding. (Philippians 4:7.)

The *mystery of God* includes how He can be in us, on earth, and in heavenly places all at the same time. It is a mystery to us how there is no time with Him. It is a mystery how He can be Father, Son, and Holy Spirit all at once, and how He can literally do something within us that causes us to be "born again" into a new race, the race of Jesus. (John 3:5,6.)

The mystery of iniquity involves how the highest being created by God before He created mankind could rebel. (Isaiah 14:12-15; Ezekiel 28:14-19.)

We tend to think that if we could have walked with Jesus on earth, much less lived with the Trinity in Heaven, we would never rebel, never have any problems, and be forever happy. We expect to live that way when we move from this natural plane to the supernatural, eternal one.

So how could someone as beautiful as the cherub that covered God's throne rebel? (Ezekiel 28:14.) How can the sin, the attitudes and behaviors of those in rebellion, ways that are totally contrary to God and His ways, still affect those who are under the New Covenant, those engrafted into the family of God?

The reason is that we live in a fallen world system, one still under the influence of "the prince of this world" (meaning "world order" or "world systems"), as Jesus called him. (John 12:31, 14:30, 16:11.)

However, we also know all authority in heaven and earth was given to Jesus.[3] (Matthew 28:18.) These two facts are contradictory, so we will never understand the mystery of iniquity until we get to Heaven — and maybe not even then!!

We must understand, however, that there is a difference between *authority* and *power*. A policeman operates in civil authority, but a criminal in a Mack truck could run over him in the street or shoot him. The power overrides his authority.

Jesus has been given all *authority* over all things. However, in the book of Hebrews, the writer says that we do not see this manifested as yet. (Hebrews 2:8.)

The enemy no longer has *authority* over Christians; but, simply because he is supernatural and we are not, he still illegally exercises *power* over our lives where we give him legal access. If he comes down the road appearing like "an 18-wheel semi," we must understand that the name of Jesus — the authority of Jesus delegated to us — can stop him in his tracks.

In the Kingdom of God, *authority* can overcome *power*, unlike the policeman in the natural world. That is because the authority we exercise, delegated to us by Jesus (Matthew 28:18-20), as well as the power the enemy exercises, both originate in an eternal, beyond-the-natural realm.

This is why Paul described our armor and our spiritual weapons in Ephesians 6:10-18. If the enemy could no longer attack us once we are born again, as some say, Paul would not have written about our defense system! Those verses were written to and for born-again people, not for the unbelievers.

These two men who demonstrated God's power in action in Old Covenant times did not have the authority of Jesus' name.

They only had obedience to God and a total commitment to speaking forth exactly what He said. Today, we have both the authority of Jesus' name and the access to His power.

Newly born-again Christians, however, do not usually "hit the ground running." As babies in Christ (1 Peter 2:2), we must be changed by the Holy Spirit from day to day into empowered soldiers for God. (2 Corinthians 3:18.) As we seek more of Him, we release more of us!

It may seem to you that you can never change — and you cannot in your own will and power. However, *anyone can change* by allowing the Holy Spirit to work in him or her.

[1]Smith, Sir William. *Smith's Bible Dictionary,* (Nashville: Thomas Nelson Publishers, 1986, orig. pub. 1831), p. 166.

[2]Ibid, p. 167.

[3]The *KJV* translates *exousia* as "power," but a better translation in that context is *authority*. The Greek word for "power" is *dunamis*, according to the late Dr. James Strong. *The New Strong's Exhaustive Concordance of the Bible,* (Nashville: Thomas Nelson Publishers, 1995), "Greek New Testament Dictionary," p. 32, #1849; p. 25, #1411.

2

Anyone Can Change

But we all, with open face (unveiled) **beholding as in a glass** (mirror) **the glory of the Lord, are changed** (being transformed) **into the same image from glory to glory, even as by the Spirit of the Lord.**[1]

2 Corinthians 3:18

What are we lacking today that only a few of us from time to time walk in the path of Elijah and Elisha?

We lack the total commitment, the total willingness to be used and to pay the price, and the total focus on God first and all else second, with self-desires at the very bottom of the list. That is a hard place to walk, but asking God for hard things will gradually bring us into a place of zero tolerance for the world.

What you have been up until now does not mean you always have to be that way or that kind of person. Your "hard thing" always will involve change in you in some way.

Every day, in every way, we are supposed to be allowing the Holy Spirit to change us to conform to the image of Christ. In fact, in another place, the Apostle Paul tells us that is a commandment, a rule of Christian life. (Romans 8:29.)

Resisting change or sitting down in the spiritual place where you are and just wanting to expand that place into different levels, will eventually result in death to your spiritual life.

What a difference fasting can make in your life.

What a difference a corporate prayer meeting, or "praying through" on your own can make.

What a difference a Holy Spirit-anointed revival can make.

What a difference a laying on of hands and/or casting out of satanic forces can make.

If you pray diligently, stay in the Word, continue to seek God's change in your life, and sit in a church where you hear the true Gospel, sooner or later a transformation will take place. Sooner or later, your mind (programmed with all of the world's thinking) will be renewed. (Ephesians 4:23.) Then you will find yourself in a new place in God.

Elijah was sent by God to show Israel the way to a new place in Him, to show them that they were in danger of dying spiritually. He was sent to show the Israelites in the nation of Israel that they were in danger of being taken over by Satan's "religion."

This period was the first and only time in the history of Israel and Judah when the covenant relationship with God had been set aside *governmentally*. This was the only period when a counterfeit religion of Satan was instituted as official policy.

During most of the history of the Hebrews who became known as the Israelites, satanic worship of idols had been present in one degree or another. At first, they were affected by idol worship in Egypt. (Exodus 32.) Then, because they did not obey God and do away with idolatry completely when they conquered Canaan (Judges 2:1-5), they slid back into idol worship.

Also, many years later, in Jeremiah's day, such worship was being carried out in the temple itself in the nation of Judah. (Ezekiel 8:16.) However, during all those years pagan worship coexisted with the worship of the true God except for the reign of Ahab. At the time of Elijah, there was no official coexistence. Baal was it.

God sent Elijah to do three things: *rebuke, reawaken,* and *restore*.

Why does God rebuke individuals or nations? Is it because he is mad at them? Is it out of wrath? No, *it is out of love* and because He still considers that person or that nation His.

When I read about Elijah, I wondered why he would be rebuking people and it be of God.

God spoke to me and said, "Nathan Simmons, I chastise those I love, and if I don't chastise you, then you are not of Me."

I found that He had already said that in His Word through the writer of Hebrews:

> **. . . My son, despise not thou the chastening of the Lord, nor faint when thou art rebuked of him: for whom the Lord loveth he chasteneth, and scourgeth every son whom he receiveth. If ye endure chastening, God dealeth with you as with sons; for what son is he whom the father chasteneth not? But if ye be without chastisement, whereof all are partakers, then are ye bastards, and not sons.**
>
> **Hebrews 12:5-8**

However, the Father does not just rebuke or chastise His children for punishment. It is to *correct* them, to put them back on the right path, His path for them. It is not to tear them down or to "whip" them, but to tear down what He is rebuking in them that is alien to Him.

Restoration Must Follow Awakening

Therefore, the second thing Elijah did was to awaken the citizens of Israel. If you do not recognize a rebuke in your life as from God, you will resist it. Some Christians even get mad at God for whatever has constituted a rebuke. Some blame the devil. They need to wake up and recognize what is happening and why.

The third thing is to restore, to complete the correction by putting a person, a family, a church, a business, or a nation back on track.

Elijah was an ordinary man used by God in extraordinary ways because he was submitted, willing, and obedient. He started out by rebuking King Ahab (1 Kings 17:1), hiding in faith and obedience (not fear) for three and one-half years of famine (1 Kings 17:3-9; Luke 4:25), and executing hundreds of false prophets in a "high noon" showdown (1 Kings 18:21-40).

Then Elijah ran from the threats of a woman. (1 Kings 19:2.) However, Queen Jezebel was not just any woman, but the daughter of the king of Sidon who was head of the worship of Baal. She supported 850 prophets of Baal and Astarte (Asherah) in the royal palace. (1 Kings 16:31, 18:19.)

In addition, she had caused the death of all but 100 of the prophets in Israel. (1 Kings 18:13.) She also influenced Ahab to not only worship Baal but to set up official shrines to that god. (1 Kings 16:31,32.)

In essence, Elijah ran from the devil in Jezebel because he had been "high" as the Lord's anointed on the mountaintop, then came down into the valley as a man. Instead of letting God handle the situation as He had on the mountain, Elijah's recourse was to run.

He fled 40 days into a different country, the southern nation of Judah. There he went to Mount Sinai, where God had disclosed Himself to Moses. (1 Kings 19:1-9; Exodus 33:21-23.) There he hid in a cave for refuge.

God's rebuke to Elijah was very tender, a "still, small voice" simply seeking to expose whatever weakness in him that had allowed him to run.

God asked, "What are you doing here, Elijah?" (1 Kings 19:9,13.)

Like most of us, this great man did not immediately confess that he had missed God. Instead, he began to defend and justify himself in self-pity.

"Hey, God, look at all I've done for You. I'm the only one in Israel You have left, and now they are trying to kill me." (1 Kings 19:10,14.)

God has never deigned to deal with excuses or self-pity. After the rebuke, God proceeded to reawaken Elijah to his calling and restore him to a new place of obedience and prophethood. God not only never sympathized with Elijah, He did not even answer his self-justifications.

He simply gave him three new assignments: Go back through Israel to Syria (Damascus) and anoint Me a king.

Secondly, anoint a king in Israel to replace Ahab.

Thirdly, find Elisha, son of Shaphat of Abelmeholah, and anoint him to replace you. (1 Kings 19:15,16.)

As an afterthought, God answered the only thing in Elijah's pity party that did not involve emotions. He gave Elijah a fact, one that probably pulled the prophet out of his depression and discouragement.

God said, "Actually, Elijah, you are not the only one I have left. There are 7,000 people in Israel who have not bowed down to Baal."

Also, Obadiah, an official of the court of Ahab, had done an extremely courageous thing before Elijah even appeared on the scene. He had hidden 100 prophets of God in two caves and fed them from the king's supplies! (1 Kings 18:13.)

Elijah through his flight had asked God for a hard thing, and he got it — a new place. He was moved from tearing down things of the enemy to setting up things for God. The things he did made a difference in the history of Israel and Judah..

Fulfilling the last assignment first, Elijah found Elisha and cast his mantle upon him as his successor. That was the first time the younger received the mantle. He had to return it, however, when he caught up with Elijah after saying good-bye to his family and farmhands. (1 Kings 19:19-21.)

The second time he got Elijah's mantle was when *he* asked for a hard thing for himself. Then he received the mantle with a double-portion anointing.

Elijah's New Place

For whatever reason — the Bible does not tell us — Elijah actually did not personally carry out the first two assignments, although he did move into international affairs as well as national after that. (1 Kings 21:17-19; 2 Kings 1:3-17.).)

His new place was mentor to Elisha and other younger prophets and elder statesmen in Israel.

Apparently, other prophets were able to operate freely and the worship of Baal was not predominant any longer because of Elijah's courage in confronting them. (1 Kings 22:7.) However, many of the prophets apparently later proved false. (1 Kings 22:8-28.) We see even thousands of years ago the truth of Jesus' words: **For many are called, but few are chosen** (Matthew 22:14).

The first assignment God gave Elijah at Mount Sinai was carried out by Elisha after Elijah was taken from him in a fiery chariot. A man named Hazael was set as king of Syria when Elisha made a visit to Damascus, having gained renown in his own right as a prophet and man of God in nations surrounding Israel.

A member of the royal court, Hazael came with presents to ask Elisha if King Benhadad would recover from an illness. When Elisha told him that God said he was to be king over Syria, Hazael killed Benhadad and mounted the throne. (2 Kings 8:7-15.)

Of course, knowing God's ways, we can think that Hazael "jumped the gun" and committed murder. If he had waited on God, he probably would have come into the kingship without murdering his predecessor.

If God anoints someone as the next pastor of a church, He is only preparing that person for his new *place*. He does not mean for him to "kill" the old pastor by taking over the church, causing a division in the congregation, or usurping authority. We need to learn to wait on God to open doors, even if He has told us what the next "door" is to be.

The second assignment God sent Elijah was fulfilled when a man named Jehu was anointed by "one of the children (sons) of the prophets" during a siege. Elisha sent that man to carry out the assignment made to Elijah.

Jehu was called to replace Ahab's son as king of Israel and to kill Ahab's descendants, ending the fourth dynasty of kings over the northern nation of Israel. (2 Kings 9:1-9.) In that case, it was the fulfillment of judgment from God ending Ahab's dynasty as He had sent Elijah to pronounce on Ahab. (1 Kings 21:17-22.)

> **. . . Thus saith the Lord God of Israel, I have anointed thee king over the people of the Lord, even over Israel. And thou shalt smite the house of Ahab thy master, that I may avenge the blood of my servants the prophets, and the blood of all the servants of the Lord, at the hand of Jezebel. For the whole house of Ahab shall perish. . . .**
>
> **2 Kings 9:6-8**

Elijah was a mentor to Elisha, as best we can tell, for at least ten years. During that time, Elisha was in *the place of a servant*. He held the pan for Elijah to wash, he emptied his chamber pot, he kept house wherever they were, and he obtained food and cooked the meals.

Where Elijah leaped on the scene a full-blown prophet, Elisha came on as a servant. During his servanthood days, he was polished by God as a stone is sandpapered smooth. That is perhaps why he never ran from danger. That is why, when Elijah died, he came into office stable, confident, and humble — no highs and lows. He had a mentor, a "father" in the Lord.

One of the most illuminating and helpful to us of the incidents involving these two men is the trip they took between Elijah's call home and the appearance of the chariot of God.

Again, we need to remember that names meant something in those days. People were given words as names that fit circumstances, characteristics, or things parents wanted them to be.

Esau, for example, is "hairy" in the Hebrew language. He was called that because he *was* hairy from the womb.[2] His twin Jacob came out of the womb holding onto Esau's heel, so he was called "the supplanter" or "the trickster," which is the word *Jacob* in Hebrew.[3]

Place names also were designated because of characteristics. Those places can be "pictures" of spiritual places, way stations, or landmarks on our spiritual journeys today. The Bible says everything in the Bible was written down as examples for God's children in later centuries.

> **These things happened to them as examples and were written down as warnings for us, on whom the fulfillment of the ages has come.**
>
> **1 Corinthians 10:11 *NIV***

[1]*The King James Version,* (Nashville: Thomas Nelson Publishers, 1994), p. 1572, center notes for verse 18.

[2]Smith, p. 179.

[3]Ibid, p. 274.

3

Places on the Road to Change

And it came to pass, when the Lord would take up Elijah into heaven by a whirlwind, that Elijah went with Elisha from Gilgal.

2 Kings 2:1

Even the place where Elijah came from tells us something. He was an inhabitant of Tishbe "in the land of Gilead." (1 Kings 17:1.) That is the only comment we have about his background. However, a common phrase from those times is "the balm of Gilead."

When I began to study Elijah, the Lord said to me, "Nathan Simmons, have you ever heard that there is a balm in Gilead?"

I said, "Yes, Master," and He said, "Elijah of Gilead was a balm to the people in Israel and at the same time a threat and terror to the kingdom of Satan."

He continued, "Everyone who has ever acted to spread My balm to My people also has been a threat and a terror to Satan. When I send people out, it is from 'Gilead,' a place in Me, to extend My balm to others."

Natural *balm* is "an aromatic gum resin" from certain trees and plants used for healing and anointing. From the camphor family, the Old Testament "balm of Gilead" refers to the juice (resin) from small evergreen trees. These trees also were native to Asia and Africa, but they only grew in Canaan in the wooded area of Gilead.[1]

The term has been extended over the years through common usage not just to mean natural healing but anything that is healing to the mind, emotions, or spirit.

For example, we say, "The peace and quiet of the countryside were balm to my soul," or "The worship service was balm to our spirits."

Therefore, Elijah was sent to spread the balm, or salve, from spiritual Gilead onto the sores of Israelites suffering under the spiritual influence of demonic forces embodied in Baal. In other words, the "balm of Gilead" can describe the presence of the Holy Spirit.

All of his life, Elijah existed to spread the balm of the Lord. When his time was over, he had trained Elisha and accomplished a lot in the natural realm.

His presence in Israel apparently had allowed Schools of Prophets, called "the sons (disciples) of the prophets" (2 Kings 2:3) to reemerge. They were first established by the Prophet Samuel (1 Samuel 19:19,20), but were not in evidence again until the days of Elijah and Elisha.

As the elder and younger prophets traveled from where they lived in Gilgal to where Elijah was carried away in a fiery chariot, their journey took them through several places. These real locations symbolize various spiritual places on any Christian's journey through life to eternity.

Gilgal: A Place To "Circle the Wagons"

Gilgal literally is "a circle of stones" or figuratively, "going around in circles." We might say it is a place to begin to conquer, a place to "circle the wagons," so to speak.

It is from a root word that means "to roll," which is the meaning God used through Joshua to remind Israel of the fact that "the reproach of Egypt" had been "rolled away" from them. (Joshua 5:9.)[2]

It is a historic place on what we would call today, "the east bank" of the Jordan. This was the territory the tribes of Reuben and Gad and half of Manasseh chose as their inheritance. It was at the south boundary of Benjamin (Joshua 18:17) and within sight of the north boundary of Judah. (Joshua 15:7.)

The southern kingdom of Judah was only made up of Judaites, Benjamites (the Apostle Paul's tribe, Romans 11:1; Philippians 3:5), and the majority of the tribe of Levites. Also, the population included a smattering of Israelites from the other ten and a half tribes [see Appendix A] that had fled to Judah in order to continue worshipping in Jerusalem after the nation divided.

What happened at Gilgal? Many things, but among the most important were these:

1. This place was Israel's first base of operations after they crossed the Jordan. (Joshua 4:19.)

2. Twelve commemorative stones were set up here when they first pitched camp as they moved in to conquer Canaan. (Joshua 4:20.)

3. The generation that grew up in the wilderness was circumcised here. (Joshua 5:7-9.)

4. The manna ceased here. (Joshua 5:12.)

5. The first Passover was held here. (Joshua 5:10.)

6. From here, Joshua led the army to surround Jericho. (Joshua 6:10,11.)

7. Tribal territories were allotted here. (Joshua 14:6.)

8. Samuel was a "circuit-riding" prophet, and this was one of his stops. (1 Samuel 7:16.) Samuel also confirmed Saul's kingship here (1 Samuel 11:14,15), and Saul also was "disenthroned" and had judgment from God passed on him here after he offered a presumptuous sacrifice in disobedience. (1 Samuel 13:8-14, 15:12-35.)

9. King David was welcomed back to his throne here by the Judaites after his son Absalom's defeated revolt. (2 Samuel 19:15,40.)

10. During the period when Israel, a people but not yet a nation, lived under judges, God's angel went up from Gilgal to pronounce sentence on Israel because of a major disobedience. (Judges 2:1-5.)

What was the disobedience? It was the failure to throw down the pagan altars of Satan and the making of treaties with the Canaanite tribes, which God had forbidden.

What were the consequences? That God would not drive out the rest of the inhabitants before them, and those inhabitants would be "thorns in their sides" and their false gods would be traps for the Israelites.

One Bible dictionary describes the place of Gilgal like this:[3]

> Gilgal thus became at once a reminder of God's past deliverance from Egypt, a token of present victory under His guidance, and the promise of inheritance yet to be gained.

We could also infer that it was the first place where God "set up camp" to begin His first nation on earth, His first step in recovering civil (governmental and societal) ground from mankind's enemy, Satan.

An angel apparently was seated there to oversee the beginning of the nation, and was sent from there to tell the people of the consequences of their disobedience — not punishment from God, but consequences. He had given them ample time to obey that directive.What then does "Gilgal" symbolize for Christians spiritually?

Gilgal is the place where everyone starts who is born again. It is the place from which you set out to "conquer the land" God has given you. On the other hand, you can choose to stay there and limit your future spiritual path.

You can choose to stay in your first "camp" and never progress any farther. A Christian ought never to forget that he or she is from "Gilgal." Always remember your "first camp," the place where you became part of God's nation and from where you glimpsed the Promised Land.

This is your birthplace in God, the place where He rolled "the reproach of Egypt" (the world) away from you when you accepted Jesus as Savior. However, unless we throw out all of the enemy's "idols," we will pursue our Christian lives hindered and fought by Satan's attitudes, behavior, and acts.

So where do we go from Gilgal? Are you happy you are saved, yet tired of going "around the mulberry bush" again and again?

Over and over and over, time and time again, do you find yourself doing the same old things, accomplishing the same old goals, with no new inspiration or new goals? Even the Apostle Paul struggled with moving to new places spiritually.

> **For I know that in me (that is, in my flesh,) dwelleth no good thing: for to will is present with me; but how to perform that which is good I find not. For the good that I would I do not: but the evil which I would not, that I do.**
>
> **Romans 7:18,19**

What place does the new Christian move into when he or she first wants to put away childish things, as Paul said? (1 Corinthians 13:11.)

From Bethel to the Jordan

What is the next step on the spiritual journey? It is usually to become a more integral part of the Body of Christ, to find a church, group, minister, or movement of which to become a part.

That "place" is called Bethel: Beth (house) plus El (God) equals "house of God." We can see why God sent Elijah and Elisha from Gilgal to Gilead to Bethel. I believe that Elisha realized the significance of traveling through the particular places they did en route to the Jordan, Elijah's final destination.

Just as with all of the places in God, it is possible to settle down and stay there. It takes remaining close to the Lord, listening to the Spirit, and asking God for a hard thing in order to move on to the next place.

It is easy to be fooled by simply expanding into different levels of the same places and thinking you are going up instead of sideways.

It is human nature not to want change and to want things to stay the same, as long as you are comfortable. This is why sometimes God allows things to happen or come into our lives that make us uncomfortable, that shake us "out of a rut."

That happened once with Moab, whom God likened to wine that settles into dregs and sours. (Jeremiah 48:11.)

The Lord said to me, "Nathan Simmons, Bethel is the house of God, but it also represents metaphorically the place of traditionalism and the place of religiosity."

Bethel is the place where, if you are not careful, you will get caught up in the "who's who" and the "what's what," the politics that develop anywhere there is an organization or a large enough group of people.

Bethel will be the place where, instead of being healed and judged ready to travel on, you end up looking at others and saying, "Why are they using him, or her, and not me? I'm just as good. I can sing or play the piano just as well. I can talk and teach as well as they can. I am being discriminated against."

This is the place where there ought to be unconditional love, where you ought to be able to come from any background and receive deliverance without questions, be accepted as a fellow citizen of the Kingdom, and be honest with everyone.

It is sad that too many churches are places of tradition and religiosity rather than love and understanding. There is no hurt like a church hurt, a choir hurt, a hurt from others who call themselves "Christian."

However, you do not have to become a part of the dwellers who have settled down in "Beth-El" and turned on others. You can be an "Elisha" who displays a contrite and humble spirit by doing whatever your hand finds to do at "Bethel" until God says it is time to move on to the next place.

The sons of the prophets at Bethel said to Elisha, "Do you know your master is going away today? He won't be around to lead you any longer. Who will you be then?" (2 Kings 2:3.)

Elisha gave them a classic answer, one which Christians ought to learn to give those who try to pull them off the path: "Hold your peace!"

In 2lst century language, that means, "Don't even go there! Mind your own business and leave mine alone."

[1]*Webster's New World Dictionary of the American Language,* (New York: Simon & Schuster, 1980, 2nd Col. Ed.), p. 108.

[2]*New Bible Dictionary,* (Leicester, England: Intervarsity Press, 1962, and Wheaton, IL: Tyndale House Publishers, Inc., 1982, 2nd. Ed.), pp. 421,422.

[3]Ibid, p. 422.

4

A Place of Adversity

And Elijah said unto him (at Bethel), **Elisha, tarry here, I pray thee; for the Lord hath sent me to Jericho. And he said, As the Lord liveth, and as thy soul liveth, I will not leave thee. So they came to Jericho.**

2 Kings 2:4

The next place Elijah said God was sending him to was *Jericho*, a valley kind of place in the natural that pictures a place on our spiritual walk.

If you look at maps of the Holy Land in the times of these two prophets, you can see that God was leading Elijah on a meandering journey to the place where he would be taken up in the chariot of God.

Why would God take their time and cause extra effort on Elijah's final journey?

I believe it was a time of testing for Elisha. You might say it was his "final examination" by his teacher concerning obedience and faithfulness. Would Elisha have received his double-portion mantle if he had gotten tired and stopped at any one of those places?

I seriously doubt it. If we get tired and weary in well-doing and sit down at any of these places on our spiritual walk, will we receive the rewards Jesus will give out on Judgment Day? (Hebrews 11:6; 2 Timothy 4:8; James 1:12; 1 Peter 5:4; Revelation 2:10.) I doubt it.

Of course, it will be wonderful just to live in Heaven. However, will some people regret all through eternity that they had nothing to lay at Jesus' feet because they became complacent or gave up too quickly? (Revelation 4:10.)

Every man's work shall be made manifest: for the day shall declare it, because it shall be revealed by fire; and the fire shall try every man's work of what sort it is. If any man's work abide which he hath built thereupon, he shall receive a reward. If any man's work shall be burned, he shall suffer loss: but he himself shall be saved; yet so as by fire.

1 Corinthians 3:13-15

As the first place the Israelites conquered in the Promised Land, Jericho exemplifies *adversity*. When Joshua surrounded the city, it was **straitly shut up** (Joshua 6:1).

No one could go in or come out, which means there was *no communication*. That is a bad place to be, where there is no communication and adversity seems to be triumphing.

This is the place where you learn God is the same in the valley as on the mountaintop. When you get out of the valley and onto the mountaintop, you will be able to look back and see how you got through the valley. You will be able to thank God for the trial through which faith develops patience. (James 1:3.)

Jericho in Hebrew is *fragrance*.[1] Walking through the valley of adversity and triumphing bring a fragrance into your Christian walk that you will not get any other way.

David said it was good to have been afflicted, because then he knew that God was able to deliver. (Psalm 119:71.)

However, I wondered why Elijah and Elisha were led into a place of no communication on Elijah's final journey.

The Lord explained, "When you first got saved, you heard Me every day. You heard through sermons in church, on the radio, or on television. I spoke to you through My Word. However, the closer you get to Me, the less I speak."

The point is that, when you were first saved, you were being trained. As you grow in the Lord, He ought not to have to keep telling you what to do as you would your five-to-ten-year-old children. Many things you learned at "Gilgal" and even at "Bethel" ought to be automatic by the time you get to "Jericho."

Once the adversity is conquered, "Jericho" becomes *a place of fragrance*. In the natural, the date palms and flowering fruit trees gave out sweet odors, watered by the Jordan, the best place on their trip so far.

Elijah probably thought his young servant would remain here and not continue across the hot plain to the muddy river. Jordan is not a beautiful, clear stream, but a muddy one, turbulent in places.

At Each Place, There Is a Choice

Notice that at each place, Elijah tested the sincerity and the commitment of Elisha by trying to get him to remain at that place instead of going on with him. At each place, however, Elisha told his master he would not leave him. (2 Kings 2:2,4,6.)

Then they went to the Jordan River, and 50 of the sons of the prophets followed them and watched from a distance. (2 Kings 2:6,7.) Elijah struck the river with his mantle, and the water parted for the two to walk over on dry ground. (2 Kings 2:8.)

On the other side, for the first time, Elijah asked what Elisha wanted him to do for him before he left. (2 Kings 2:9.) He had spent the first part of the trip testing him on his tenacity, patience, and persistence in seeking God.

As Elisha had "stayed the course," now he could choose his reward. He could ask Elijah for whatever he wanted. Would it be prosperity, a long life, wisdom, protection from his enemies? It is significant that this final discussion between the elder and the younger prophets occurred at the edge of the Jordan River.

Jordan means "the descender" in Hebrew, because it winds 200 miles downstream to the Dead Sea.[2] It is the lowest depression on earth. However, in the Bible it represents, not so much "down" as *across*. It also is known as "the great divide."

The River Jordan has become symbolic of the end of natural life where we cross over to the other side. We descend into death, the lowest point in life, in order to ascend into Heaven — if we are born again as children of God..

The Jordan River also is a metaphor of a place in our spiritual walk where we descend in order to ascend. We move from a place of serving others, a place of humility, to a place of ministry, a place of "elevation" in the spirit, a place of understanding.

Notice that the two men of God were taken to the Jordan from Bethel (the house of the Lord) and then through Jericho (adversity). If you are truly faithful in your assignment in a church or ministry, then do not be surprised if adversity comes when you are at the point of crossing Jordan to the next place in your spiritual life.

However, we will not make it at the Jordan if the place of servanthood has not become an integral part of our beings. If we have only pretended to be good helpers to others, if we have even inwardly grumbled and complained, then we have not truly developed a servant's heart.

Jesus said those who would be in the highest positions in the Kingdom must have learned how to be good servants. (Luke 22:25-30.)

> **. . . If any man desire to be first, the same shall be last of all, and servant of all.**
>
> **Mark 9:35**

The highest reward we can receive after "crossing the Jordan" to the other side of eternity will be Jesus' words in Matthew 25:23:

> **. . . Well done, good and faithful *servant;* thou hast been faithful over a few things, I will make thee ruler over many things: enter thou into the joy of thy lord.**

Today, in a culture of instant everything, of instant gratification of our desires, of having practically anything we want available on "terms," we do not want to hear messages of patience, tenacity, and humbling ourselves before others. All we want to hear are miracles, instant healing, and unworked for prosperity.

We want to hear that we are "the heads and not the tails" (Deuteronomy 28:13), which is true concerning our position in Christ, but blessings in the Kingdom are not always material.

We have limited the God of Abraham, Isaac, and Jacob to the place of a permissive "daddy" who only exists to shower blessings on us. We do not want to hear about a Father who reigns in justice and power and chastises us for our good when we need it.

If everything God has given you was taken away, as happened to Job (Job 1:12), would you still serve Him? Remember that God spoke of Job *before his testing* as **My servant** and held him up to Satan as a perfect example. (Job 1:8.)

Do you think the Almighty God, who knows the future from the very beginning, would have allowed Job's testing had He not already known this man "perfect in all his ways" (Job 1:8) would pass the test?

Nevertheless what God knew, Job still had to make the right choices as we all do. Any Christian who ever made a wrong choice when he or she came to the place of "Jordan" had the same opportunity to make the right one.

Are you only serving God for what He can give you, for a car, or a house, or even a husband or wife?

Jesus said:

For what shall it profit a man, if he shall gain the whole world, and lose his own soul?

Mark 8:36

Once Elisha's character was strengthened by passing through all these places, he received the hard thing for which he asked and moved to a place we all would like to be: *the place of understanding*. No more wondering why this or that, but revelation as to our callings, our positions, and who we truly are in Christ.

[1]Smith, p. 290; Strong's "Hebrew Dictionary," p. 60, #3405.
[2]Ibid, p. 319; New Bible Dictionary, pp. 615-617.

5

A Place of Understanding

And he took the mantle of Elijah that fell from him, and smote the waters, and said, Where is the Lord God of Elijah? and when he also had smitten the waters, they parted hither and thither: and Elisha went over.

2 Kings 2:14

We might say Elisha had served an apprenticeship, not even an assistantship, for at least ten years. Now at the Jordan River, *when he asked for a hard thing* and persisted until he got it, he was ordained into his own prophet's office.

The *mantle* stands for his ordination. Incidentally, Elijah had taken Elisha full circle back to the land of Gilead, across the Jordan (Trans-Jordan), which apparently was Elijah's birthplace. Elijah was a "Tishbite," or from Tishbe, located in Gilead.

I am convinced in this last hour that many of God's children are not in a place of understanding. Many Christians, especially in the prosperous countries, have "made camp" in Gilgal, Bethel, and Jericho. Few have crossed the great divide between "religion" and true fellowship with God.

In the last century, God brought the Body of Christ into a place of fragrance, of signs and wonders, a place where we are the "head and not the tail," a place where our dependence should be totally on God.

You will not reach a place of understanding until everyone who knows you or sees you can say, "Look at his, or her, life. He has something we do not. That must be God. He must have crossed the Jordan and returned with a mantle of anointing."

This place is so wonderfully profound, because it has nothing to do with your genealogy, nothing to do with your environment or education, nothing to do with who you think you are — but only to do with who God is and who you are in Him.

In a place of understanding, we "know that we know" that everything and anything we have was given to us by God, naturally as well as spiritually. This is a wonderful place to be, a special place, and it is marked by humility, not superiority.

At the Jordan, the sons of the prophets who had been at Jericho followed the two men and watched from a distance. Those who "stand afar off" (2 Kings 2:7) and watch what happens when you return from crossing the Jordan to take up your mantle of service need your example to cross their own "Jordans."

Surrounding those watching, who are also children of God but still on a journey, is a world of degradation, a world of paganism, the world of the fallen Adamic race.

This is a time when people are trying to lead one another instead of looking to God, a time when the majority of the world's population do not believe in any God or believe in many gods. You could call the beginning of the 21st century a time of "the blind leading the blind" (Luke 6:39), a time when many are falling into ditches on the right and on the left of truth.

However, it seems a contradiction but this also is a time when more people are coming to the true God than ever before. It is a time of taking the Gospel to the whole world. The increase in born-again people is in what we call "the third-world countries."

Christianity in western countries is decreasing, yet we have the most preachers, evangelists, churches, and radio and TV ministries of anywhere in the world.

The hardest people to witness to or to tell about God are not the people who have never known God, but those who have heard much about Him and hardened their hearts. Also, those who have been so "brainwashed" with a false god that their hearts are hardened.

The hardest people I have found to talk to about God are backslidden "PKs" (preachers' kids). Try to tell them what God can do, and they say, "Been there, done that. Don't bother me."

When you come to the real place of understanding, God has given you a hard thing. You begin to face impossible things, but a true understanding of God will enable you to overcome, to cross back over the river, to say, "Where is the Lord God of Elijah who will do the same things through me?" (2 Kings 2:14.)

God is calling His people to rebuke sins, to reawaken others of His children, and to restore them in order to be a strong presence in a dangerous time in history for the Body of Christ.

When Elisha took up Elijah's mantle and went back across the Jordan to begin his life's work, he did not take his place or his assignment lightly. Immediately, he was confronted with things to overcome.

After at least ten years of living in "the balm of Gilead," Elisha came to a crossroads in his life. Would he be content to bask in the Spirit and do some things against the enemy? Or would he ask for a hard thing and be moved to a different place?

The first thing he had to overcome was the reputation he had with the sons of the prophets. They still saw him as Elijah's servant not a prophet in his own right. They thought they had as much understanding in God as he did, although they had remained in Jericho.

Friends Can Hinder You

These prophets came to meet Elisha and admitted that **the spirit of Elijah doth rest on Elisha**, and they bowed down before him in respect. (2 Kings 2:15,16.) However, did they really believe what they had seen? Apparently not.

The second thing they said was, "Hey, man, maybe God dropped Elijah's body on some mountain or in some valley. Let's go and look for him."

Elisha forbade them to look until they made him ashamed. They acted as if he did not want to find Elijah's body and give it a proper burial. So he finally told them all to go and look. After 50 of them had looked within a three-day radius and found nothing, they returned to Jericho where he was waiting for them.

Then he said, "I told you so. Maybe you guys will learn to believe that I know from God what I speak." (2 Kings 2:16-18.)

Sometimes your family members or your closest friends will not believe that you are hearing from God. Sometimes they try to hinder you by putting you on "guilt trips" that you should be doing this or doing that. All of the time, you know you are not supposed to be doing that.

The third thing involved the city elders of Jericho who said, in essence, "Let us see what you can do. Prove yourself, Elisha!"

They said, "We have a good town, but the water is bad which makes the ground barren." (2 Kings 2:19-22.)

That was the same thing as in Jesus' day when the scribes and Pharisees kept asking Him for a "sign" to prove He was Messiah. (Matthew 12:38,39, 16:1-4.) Jesus did signs and wonders, but not on demand or to "prove" anything for skeptics.

One time, however, He did say, "If you can't believe My words, at least believe what I do." (John 14:11.) However, He was teaching His disciples when He said that, not unbelievers such as the Pharisees, the "religious" folks.

Elisha cast salt, which stands for permanence and incorruption and was part of all offerings to God (Leviticus 2:13), into the spring from which the waters flowed — and the waters were "healed." (2 Kings 2:22.)

If Jericho was such a "place of fragrance," why was the land barren and the water "bad"? That actually was Elisha's first assignment from the Lord, to make bad waters good so that the place could once again become fragrant.

Joshua had cursed Jericho after conquering it, and apparently both the people who continued to live there and the land had suffered since then. (Joshua 6:26.) Now it was God's mercy and goodness to show that places, as well as people, could be restored. A new era had dawned on Jericho.

When we cross back over the Jordan with our "mantles" from the Lord, we should expect to be confronted by those who try to pull us into good works to prove who we are. Expect to be met by those who want you to *prove* you are in a different place.

Will you have "salt" to heal the waters of dead churches?

Will you have the discernment to discern God-assigned works from good works and the salt of the covenant of the Spirit from presumption?[1]

Backtracking on his path with Elijah from Gilgal in Gilead, Elisha went from Jericho to Bethel, the place of tradition and religiosity.

Why did he go back? Was he losing ground and going back to the past? No, he was going "back to his future" by way of his past in order to blaze a path for others. He walked through his past showing what a person can become in God if he moves on to a different place.

At Bethel, Elijah met another kind of confrontation, one that stands for the fiery darts of the enemy. Strongholds of the enemy often exist alongside traditional religion that has not had its waters purified by the salt of the Spirit.

The demonic forces of the enemy were typified by a large group of teenage (or even young adult) hoodlums. The *King James Version* says "little children." However, the Hebrew word more correctly means "youths."[2] They taunted Elisha by calling him "old bald head." Oddly enough, the older Elijah apparently had plenty of hair while the younger man was bald.

Was Elisha vain or proud? No, he knew the attack was against him as a prophet of God. To let it go would hinder his standing in the community as a man of God.

On your way from Bethel to the place God has called you to serve, you must understand when humility is called for and when standing up for God is called for. That is part of walking in the new "place of understanding."

The street gangs must have heard about Elijah's being taken up, because they were daring Elisha to "go up," meaning, "Why don't you go up in a fiery chariot also?" (2 Kings 2:23.)

Their insults ultimately were aimed at God, not His prophets, and amounted to blasphemy. However, this street gang put Elisha's whole prophetic ministry in danger.[3]

When the two bears appeared and mauled 42 of the youths, we can see what a large mob the enemy had instigated to riot against the newly ordained man of God.

That was not a good time for the young men to come against God. That was not a good time in the history of the Israelites to be part of a mob attacking God's man. That is because He was showing His presence strongly in an effort to warn the northern nation of Israel that its continuing existence was hanging in the balance.

Do you think there might have been a youth or two who was only "going along with the crowd," who was only staying in good standing with his peers? The crowd is not always right. The majority may win, but it is not always right.

Be careful not to remain in a place where your "yokefellows" are coming against God. The "bears" may come against you as well as them.

A Place of Yokefellows

Be careful with whom you associate. *Association leads to assimilation*, or as the old saying goes, "Birds of a feather flock together."

The minor prophet Amos, who lived after Elijah and Elisha, put it this way: **Can two walk together, except they be agreed?** (Amos 3:3).

There are two options open to anyone who finds himself in a church or part of a group made up of hypocrites. One is to rise up in righteous indignation and leave the group. The other is to become a part of them.

As I pointed out earlier in this book, society in America today bears a close resemblance to that of Israel in Elisha's time, 800 years before Jesus.

Paganism, occultism, and atheism/secularism are at least equal in strength to Christianity if not more prevalent in some areas. A strong move is underway to make the worship of many gods (pluralism) the "official" religion.

The popular thinking is that all are simply "different ways to God," equally valid, and even satanism has a "right" to be in the public forum.

"Bethel," the organized, institutional Church of today, contains young people brought up in local churches who have never been saved or are in backslidden conditions. Many of them have no respect for authority and little awe of God.

Why should they not make fun of televangelists and pastors when they hear the ridicule every day on television, both news and entertainment programs?

Where is the "salt" in our churches?

Where are those who are being "salt and light" (Matthew 5:13) in society?

Where are those leaders like Elisha who will condemn blasphemy wherever it occurs?

After passing through testing of his commitment, through confrontation, and through attacks, Elisha returned to Samaria, the scene of his ministry. Notice he did not go back to Gilgal in Gilead, the beginning place.

He had served notice on demonic forces as well as people that he would not put up with disrespect for God. Young people brought up to follow God and not the world can have an important effect on society and the Church. We need to give them the courage to be different than their peers.

It seems to me the Church today is missing the "mothers" and "fathers" in Israel, the saints who can look at young people's lives and see where God wants to take them.

Let us leave Elisha and travel forward 100 years[4] to take a look at the southern kingdom of Judah in a time when a youth, who was different from his peers, led the nation into alignment with God's ways.

[1]Freeman, James M. *The New Manners and Customs of the Bible*, (North Brunswick, NJ: Bridge-Logos Publishers, 1998), p. 143.

[2]Strong's "Hebrew Dictionary," p. 56, #3206.

[3]Dates taken from the chart of kings of Israel and Judah in *Zondervan's NIV Bible Commentary* by Kenneth L. Barker & John Kohlenberger III, consulting editors, (Grand Rapids: Zondervan Publishing House, 1994), pp. 580-583.

[4]Ibid, p. 539.

6

A Place of Alignment

Then all the people of Judah took Uzziah, who was sixteen years old, and made him king in the room (place) **of his father Amaziah . . . and as long as he sought the Lord, God made him to prosper.**

2 Chronicles 26:1,5

Sin is not only an old-fashioned word today, but one that no longer means anything. Instead of sins, even Christians say they have "problems." Sin does not need exposing. Everyone knows exactly where they are and what they are doing.

Adulterers, homosexuals, addicts of all kinds, along with those who cheat on their income tax and bring home supplies from the office, sit in church unconvicted of sin.

We need Elijahs to rebuke, reawaken, and restore Christians in this country.

We need many Christians to rise up and ask God for hard things. America needs Christians to join as "fellowlaborers" in the kingdom, not to be "yokefellows" with the world.

We need to remember that there is a book in Heaven where everything we do and say is written down. (Revelation 21:27, 22:19.) Children of God will be judged for their works, while sinners will be judged on whether they have received Jesus or not.

Every day in every way, we are preparing ourselves to live eternally with Jesus. If we are not walking His way and eliminating everything from our lives, our thoughts, and our behavior that is not of God, how can we be assimilated into the heavenly society?

Sin is "missing the mark."[1]

Sin is even thinking something that is not of God.

This youth who lived a century after Elisha began as a good example to the people of God. His name was Uzziah, but he is called Azariah in the book of 2 Kings.

Uzziah was the king of Judah whose reign ended shortly after the beginning of the ministry of the prophet Isaiah. Perhaps the most well-known of the references to Uzziah involves Isaiah's "ordination," the time when God called him, and he said, "Here am I, send me."

> **In the year that king Uzziah died I saw also the Lord sitting upon a throne, high and lifted up, and his train filled the temple.**
>
> **Isaiah 6:1**

This story, unfortunately, does not have a happy ending. However, it begins well, it begins right on target, it begins with a youth brought up by a father and grandfather to align the people he governed with God.

This was about 50 years before the northern kingdom of Israel was overrun by Assyria. Judah had remained closer to covenant worship throughout its history than Israel. Perhaps this was because Jerusalem, the capital of Judah, was so reminiscent of the judges, the early prophets, and temple worship.

Ahab, the object of Elijah's preaching, had been the son of Omri. King Omri built Samaria as a new capital for the northern kingdom. It had no temple to Jehovah, no high priest, and no strict worship, but the nation was populated by many more Israelites than Judah.

Sixteen is a wonderful age. Elisha had lived into the reign of Uzziah's father, and his influence had affected Judah as well as

Israel. The years when Uzziah reigned in Judah and Jeroboam II reigned in Israel are known as the "Indian summer" of the nation of Israel.

Jonah, Amos, and Hosea all were prophets sent mostly to Israel during that time, as were Elijah and Elisha, which tells us Israel was farther from God and in more danger of judgment than Judah.

From Solomon's son, Rehoboam, most of Judah's kings had kept the nation aligned with God for the most part. However, idolatry crept in to a greater or lesser extent depending on who was king. Actually, idolatry in the united kingdom of Israel began in King Solomon's day.

The wisest king massed so many wives and concubines that, to keep peace, he allowed them to worship pagan gods. Eventually, he began to worship them himself. (1 Kings 11:1-8.) Idolatry on his part was the cause of God determining to take the kingdom away from his son, Rehoboam, which resulted in Israel being divided into Israel and Judah. (1 Kings 11:9-12.)

Choices Result in Alternate Routes

In studying the period of the kings of Israel and Judah, I wondered why time after time the kings took alternate routes. Some would be holy and move after the things of God, some would be out-and-out wicked, and others were sort of half-and-half.

God said to me, "The result (of their choices) was that they would never become worshipped as individuals."

David, Solomon's father and the united kingdom's second king, was the closest to being revered down through the ages, but a lot of his fame was that his line out of all the lines of Judah was to be the line of Messiah.

If you look at David's life, you can tell he made several major wrong choices and was not in a position to inspire worship, only respect. However, he was one of the best examples of leadership that Israel ever had with no hint of idolatry but with a heart that followed steadfastly after God. (Acts 13:22.)

If the leaders of any nation are into idolatry, then at least some of the people will follow.

If the leaders of the United States are into sin and do not hold the standard for the God of our fathers, then the people will follow them into anti-Christian ways.

This 16-year-old king began his reign dealing with "a hard thing." He warred against the Philistines, the Arabians (nomadic descendants of Esau), and the Ammonites and other tribes in surrounding areas who had not been driven out in Joshua's day.

His fame spread up into Israel and Syria and down into Egypt. He listened to a prophet named Zechariah (not the one of the book by that name, who lived much later). We are not told anything about this Zechariah, except that he **had understanding in the visions of God** (2 Chronicles 26:5) and was Uzziah's counselor.

This prophet had moved into *the place of understanding*.

We are not told anything about Uzziah's mother, but her name was Jecoliah (2 Chronicles 26:3), which in Hebrew is "She who saw that God was able." Also, she was from Jerusalem, not from one of the heathen foreign nations around Judah.

Do you think she got that name like we would say Mary or Joan or Debra? No, her name meant something, even if only to her parents who called her that. Each time anyone spoke to that woman, he or she was saying, "She has seen that God is able." Her name was a constant reminder to her husband and son.

Instead of holding our young people to a standard, we consider their "rights" and preach "God understands." God never understands sin nor condones it. Most of those ministers today who preach sermons that are almost licenses to sin have some sin in their own lives that they do not want to let go.

They say glibly, "Everyone has sinned and come short of the glory of God (Romans 3:23), so I am no different."

That verse means everyone needs to be born again. It is not and excuse for sinful ways and thoughts *after* salvation. The Apostle Paul was saying that we all have come short of righteousness and must be justified through the free gift of God's grace through Jesus.

Every now and then, we all need someone to tell us, "That is not the right way. You need to repent and straighten up."

Uzziah's mother had to have made some deposits in his life. She had to have known that her responsibility was not just birthing this child in the natural, but birthing his destiny in God.

Uzziah's father, Amaziah, also set him an example. He had started out doing right in the sight of God. However, Amaziah turned away in his later years — just as his son was to do — and was killed in a conspiracy against his reign.

We need people who will be a guideline, a measuring stick, *all* of our lives in order that we can see we are on the right course.

When he became king, Uzziah built towers at strategic places in Jerusalem and fortified them. He also built towers in the desert and dug a lot of wells for the sake of his cattle. We are told that he loved farming or gardening. (2 Chronicles 26:9,10.)

He sounds like a peace-loving man. Yet, he knew how important it was to have a good army and good defenses. He had "a host of fighting men" who went out by companies to defend Judah on various fronts. He made sure his fighting men were well-equipped, and he even had catapults built. (2 Chronicles 26:11-15.)

In other words, like Solomon, he was ahead of his time in inventions and knowledge. Both men were not just intelligent above the average, *they listened to God above the average*.

This young man was so wonderfully aligned with the ways of God that he could deal with foreign nations and be respected. He not only built towers and commissioned "cunning" (smart, inventive) men to devise weapons, but like David, he earned the respect of "mighty men of valor." Soldiers joined his armies by the thousands. (2 Chronicles 26:12,13.)

Apparently — reading between the lines — he consulted Zechariah periodically to make sure he was still aligned with God's will. (2 Chronicles 26:5.).)

I believe he would say, "Zechariah, did I do what God wanted me to do?"

And I believe the prophet would see a vision of what he was to do next. He would confirm the things he saw God doing through this young man. When the enemy's troops would come in like a flood, Uzziah was ready to lift a standard against them. (Isaiah 59:19.)

Uzziah was a leaders' leader, because he allowed God to direct his ways. He knew how to take insecure men and give them the security of knowing who they were in God.

Like his forefather David, he stood out in a crowd. King Saul stood out in a crowd also, but it was because of his height in the natural. He stood "head and shoulders" above most men of his day. (1 Samuel 10:23.) David stood out in a crowd because of his spiritual height, and so did Uzziah.

When he remained aligned with God's ways and will, when he obeyed God, *God prospered his way*. (2 Chronicles 26:5.) When he kept himself in the presence of Almighty God, the Creator made a way out of no way for him. When he did not see a way out, when he did not know how something could be done, when he had no power or might of his own, he went to God.

Uzziah's Downfall

As long as he sought God through Zechariah, God prospered his way. In the days of the Old Covenant, God's children generally had to go to him through a king, a priest, or a prophet.

Under Jesus, our eternal Mediator (1 Timothy 2:5; Hebrews 12:24), each of us can go to Him directly. We have the Holy Spirit living within us for fast and easy communication.

As long as he was small in his own eyes, as long as he was humble, Uzziah prospered. Humbleness is something you choose, not something God does for you. You do not want God to humble you! That is when pride goes before a fall, and destruction follows. (Proverbs 16:18.)

When you recognize that it is through no goodness of your own, but the grace and mercy of God that you have made it this far, then you are in alignment with God.

You had better remember that whatever God does for you is for His glory, not because you are so smart or so special or so good. God even reminded the Hebrews who became Israel through Abraham, Isaac, and Jacob that He had not chosen them because of their own qualifications. He chose them because He loved them and because of His oath to their fathers, Abraham, Isaac, and Jacob. (Deuteronomy 7:7.)

Over and over, God reminds us through Scripture directly and indirectly that, for His glory, He chooses the foolish things of the earth to confound the wise. (1 Corinthians 1:27,28.)

God has used the well-educated, like the Apostle Paul, and the very intelligent, like King Solomon. More often, however, He has used those whom the world can see are not doing great things in themselves. Peter and the other apostles were uneducated and, perhaps, most of them were not very smart.

If you begin to brag about how sanctified you are, how well you fulfill the Christian walk, then your righteousness in Jesus becomes self-righteousness, which looks to God like "filthy rags." (Isaiah 64:6.)

No matter what place of spiritual progress you are in — "Gilgal, Bethel, Jericho, or Samaria" — it is most important of all to stay in *a place of alignment with God.* That is a bottom-line place that undergirds all the rest. You might say that is a "Jerusalem place," a foundational place for all the rest.

We have had some leaders today like Uzziah, born in "Jerusalem" and reared in the ways of God with godly fathers and mothers. Yet down the road, after a lot of success in "Samaria," they began to take the glory to themselves. And great has been the downfall thereof.

The moral of Uzziah's life is this: *Do not stop seeking God.* Do not ever move off the foundation of "Jerusalem."

[1]*Zondervan's NIV Bible Commentary*, p. 662.

7

The Foundational Place

But when he was strong, his heart was lifted up to his destruction: for he transgressed against the Lord his God, and went into the temple of the Lord to burn incense upon the altar of incense.

2 Chronicles 26:16

Uzziah made Jerusalem such a place that all Judaites could find whatever they needed there. They could withstand sieges, if the enemy got that far into Judah.

When I saw all that, I asked God, "What is it about Jerusalem?"

He said, "Jerusalem was the place of foundation building."

Jerusalem was God's place from the time of David. We can even see the spiritual picture of the city-to-be when Abraham met Melchizedek there before Isaac and Jacob were even born. We can see the spiritual picture of the place long before Jacob's sons were born, those who became the nations of Israel and Judah. (Genesis 14:18.)

One of the names of Jerusalem was Zion. Today, spiritual Zion is the foundational place for us, the "Jerusalem place" founded on the Rock, Christ Jesus, according to the Apostle Paul. (1 Corinthians 10:4.)

The thing we want to learn from Uzziah is not so much starting out in a place of alignment with God *but how to remain there*. When we cross our "Jordan," pass through "Jericho" and

"Bethel," we want to go to "Samaria" (the world) *to do the will of God*, not to become so prideful or so busy doing things *for* Him that we stop seeking Him.

The Holy Spirit said to me when I began the teaching in this book, "Let My people know that, no matter what I have done for them in the past, no matter what they have accomplished, no matter how successful they have been in life, *they should not stop seeking Me*."

He said that Christians have come to a place where they are taking things for granted, even if only in the very small areas of life. For example, there used to be a time when we would stop and pray protection over our homes and our cars, and plead the blood of Jesus over our families.

Now, we have good alarm systems, neighborhood watches, and perhaps live in quiet neighborhoods. So we think there is no reason to "plead the blood" over us. We let our children go off to school without prayer, where in past times, we had family prayer and even anointed their heads with oil.

There was a time in our individual lives as we walked with God that we believed Him for every little thing. When we were called on in church to read the scriptures, we got up feeling like ministers of the Gospel. We were nervous and asked people to pray for us.

Now we are so sure of ourselves that we think we "have it made in the shade." Many of us no longer depend on the anointing of God.

Deacons and elders do not cry out to God for guidance so much anymore.

Musicians in our churches are not anointed or filled with the Spirit, but we applaud them because they can play chords and hit drum licks that make people shout.

Perhaps when you first came to God, you did not have anything, and you depended on Him for everything. You sought Him for the least little thing. You believed him for a job.

You knew you were not qualified, but you said, "God, if You will just give me this job, I will go to school for training or do whatever I have to do to make good at it."

Uzziah had his armies, his weaponry, his towers of defense, and his gardens, herds, and fields to provide food. He had wealth and fame. Apparently, at that point he stopped seeking God and began to take credit for all his wonderful accomplishments.

He began to feel that all of it was about him. In short, he forgot the prophet as intercessor, the priest as mediator of sacrifices, and began to think he, the king, was all there was. He did something that not only put an end to his kingship but to his life.

What Was Uzziah's Sin?

What did he do that was so awful, so blasphemous, so much against God?

Uzziah offered a sacrifice that was not his to offer. He stood in a place that was not his to stand in. He usurped a place reserved for priests who had been cleansed, who had no blood of warfare on their hands, and who spent much of their time in worship to God.

In other words, he became presumptuous against God in spite of those around him who tried to save him.

Azariah, the high priest, and fourscore lesser priests got between Uzziah and the altar, trying to talk him into turning away from this course of action. The Bible calls them "valiant men," because the king could have had them executed.

It takes valiant men to stand up for what is right in any situation, whether or not they might be killed.

And they withstood Uzziah the king, and said unto him, It appertaineth not unto thee, Uzziah, to burn incense unto the Lord, but to the priests the sons of Aaron, that are consecrated to burn incense: go out of the sanctuary; for thou hast trespassed; neither shall it be for thine honour from the Lord God.

2 Chronicles 26:18

Did Uzziah repent and change his attitude? No, he did not. He perhaps did not know history well enough to remember what happened when Saul, Israel's first king, became presumptuous and disobedient. (1 Samuel 15:17-23.) Instead, Uzziah added insult to injury. He became angry.

Then Uzziah was wroth, and had a censer in his hand to burn incense: and while he was wroth with the priests, the leprosy even rose up in his forehead before the priests in the house of the Lord, from beside the incense altar.

2 Chronicles 26:19

Then not only did the priests actually "thrust" him out of the temple, but Uzziah himself *hurried* to get out. However, it was too late.

Consequences had arrived, and Uzziah lived as a leper the rest of his life. What a comedown! (2 Chronicles 26:20-23.)

No matter how much you have done for God or how high you get in the world or the Kingdom, *stay out of presumption.*

The higher you go, the lower you should stay — on your knees. Notice that the same place where Uzziah was anointed and appointed king is the same place where he sinned out of pride and self-will.

After God set him down, he was still king. However, he was dysfunctional. He could no longer operate in his office as king. That is a hard place, totally out of alignment with God, to have a title, have a position, have a wonderful previous reputation as God's man, and no longer be able to function.

Whatever you do, stay on the foundation and keep seeking God. The foundation of "Jerusalem" is what all of the other places in your spiritual growth are based on. Without a firm foundation, the "house" of your life is built on sand. Storms, floods, and even termites can eat away at everything that is not built on the "place of Jerusalem."

Looking at the state of the Church in America today, it appears to me that many Christians and even local churches are on the verge of having become so "high" in the Jerusalem place that they are in danger of falling like Uzziah.

The Apostle Peter warned of the folly of slipping into this kind of pride:

> **. . . God resisteth the proud and giveth grace to the humble. Humble yourselves therefore under the mighty hand of God, that he may exalt you in due time.**
>
> **1 Peter 5:5,6**

God had exalted Uzziah because of his obedience. However, the king took the glory to himself. Somehow today, we see the mainstream Church decaying because of not giving God the glory. Instead, we tend to credit programs, activities, and even great ministry for building the Kingdom.

In prosperous times, we tend to forget the things God did when we could do nothing. We are prone to forget the times when our backs were against the wall, and God stepped in to say, "Stand back and let me do it, because I am God."

Uzziah was ahead in his walk with God by being able to begin in "Jerusalem," but instead of bringing humility, his position and place tempted him into the sin of pride. King Solomon, called "wiser than all men" (1 Kings 4:31), had much to say about pride.

> **Pride goeth before destruction, and an haughty spirit before a fall. Better it is to be of an humble spirit with the lowly, than to divide the spoil with the proud.**
>
> **Proverbs 16:18,19**

However, we also can see from Bible history that Solomon did not really heed his own warnings, although he never fell into the arrogance of Uzziah.

The best way for a Christian to keep the right perspective is to seek God until there comes the revelation that we are creatures made *and owned* by God, the Creator, the Owner of the universe and all that is in it.

Unless we come to see the reality that we are allowed the right to make choices about our lives — even the choice to join Satan in hell — by the grace of the All-Powerful One, we become arrogant. The Adamic nature with which every human being is born causes each of us to live in unreality.

If you have any doubt as to the effectiveness of the Church, look at a recent survey done by George Barna Associates [see Appendix B]:

The majority of some 6,000 people surveyed claimed to be born again but were not certain that the Bible is true, that Jesus lived a sinless life, and that the devil is a real being and not just a symbol of evil. In fact, most thought the idea that the devil is a real being who can affect people's lives is "hogwash."

The majority of Christians surveyed in earlier studies could not say who preached the Sermon on the Mount! Those who did hazard a guess tended to say "Moses."

This is the only country in the world which began with freedom to study the Bible, to attend the church of one's choice, and to teach morality without government interference. In the past half-century, Christians have allowed the United States to become more like Samaria, capital of Israel in Ahab's time, than the "Jerusalem Place" it was originally.

The High Places Must Be Destroyed

Notice that "Jerusalem" is the foundational place, but the Christian walk usually does not begin there. Most of us must first become children of God through Jesus then walk through the other places such as Gilgal and Jericho to get to the foundation.

Recent additions to the Kingdom actually have entered from "Samaria," the place of paganism and occultism. Are we helping those converts reach Jerusalem? Are our churches teaching them about the Solid Rock, Jesus, who *is* the Foundation?

Even most Christians subconsciously believe the illusion, or delusion, that we are independent creatures, that we are "as God" (Genesis 3:5) and have ultimate control over our lives and destinies. We somehow feel we are "doing God a favor" by letting Him save us, by choosing Him.

There is no solid rock foundation beneath us until we come to the realization of who God is and who we are in relation to Him. That realization will bring true humility and allow us to live in "the Jerusalem Place."

Now let's skip over the next two generations in Judah when Uzziah's son and grandson reigned. The son, Jotham, followed in his father's early years of "doing what was right in the sight of God." (2 Kings 15:34.) He lived out his reign without falling into presumption, but he did not destroy the places where worship of other gods continued.

Our lives will not be established on a firm foundation as long as we do not "pull down" any strongholds of the enemy in our lives. Allowing those things to remain that are not like Jesus in word, deed, or belief sows the seeds of defeat in our lives.

Jotham allowed those places to remain, and his son Ahaz, Uzziah's grandson, was pulled off by paganism into *not* doing what was right in the eyes of the Lord. (2 Kings 16:1-4.) As the leader of the nation, he opened the door to the enemy which was Assyria in his day.

Ahaz took the things dedicated to God and turned them over as bribes to the king of Assyria who offered sacrifices to idols on the altar of God. (2 Kings 16:7-18.) Ahaz and a large number of the people of Judah were more afraid of the devil and his representatives than of the Living God.

This is what can happen to anyone of us who allows the "high places" of the world to remain in our lives. Our examples affect the lives of our children, pastors' examples affect the lives of their congregations, and godly leaders determine the direction of a nation.

Looking at the life of Hezekiah is once again "going back to the future."

8

Going Back to the Future

Now it came to pass . . . that Hezekiah the son of Ahaz king of Judah began to reign . . . He trusted in the Lord God of Israel; so that after him was none like him among all the kings of Judah, nor any that were before him.

2 Kings 18:1,5

After Ahaz, Judah got a king who was more upright in the eyes of God than any of his predecessors. Hezekiah, Uzziah's great-grandson, had the advantage of a strong mentor — the prophet Isaiah.

However, Hezekiah's reign over Judah coincided with the final downfall of the northern nation of Israel. The warnings of Elijah, Elisha, Amos, Hosea, all of Israel, and others like Micah and Isaiah, who were of Judah, had gone unheeded.

And the Lord rejected all the seed of Israel, and afflicted them, and delivered them into the hand of spoilers, until he had cast them out of his sight.

2 Kings 17:20

The ten tribes of Israel were taken into exile and disappeared from the pages of the Bible. [The nation of Judah also later was conquered but was restored to become known in Jesus' day as Judea.]

Once when I was praying, the Lord said to me, "Prophecy is nothing but going back to the future," and I was puzzled.

"Now, Lord, wait a minute," I said, "what are You trying to tell me? People are going to think I am crazy if I say that. You need to explain it to me."

I spent about another hour praying in the Spirit, then the Lord spoke again and said, "Get up. You have to shut up and listen if you want to hear what I am going to tell you."

Have you ever heard the Lord say to you, "Shut up and listen"? The Bible says His sheep know His voice (John 10:27), but if you do not learn to listen, you will never hear His voice enough to recognize it.

So I got up off my knees, sat down in a chair, and began to listen.

The Lord said, "Nathan, everything I have to say now, I have already said in the past. The reason it seems new to you is that you did not know Me before, nor did you know My ways or My plan."

So many times God must take us back to where we first started in order to bring us on to where He wants us to be.

We are not told how Hezekiah became a righteous king after the example of his father. His grandfather and great-grandfather had presided over Judah in prosperous times, and one commentator says:[1]

> The luxury and ease of the time of Uzziah and Jotham had produced a spiritual indolence in Judah that would allow Ahaz's open sin to flourish.

We are not told what caused Hezekiah to rebel against the open sin, paganism, and permissiveness of his father's reign. We are just told what he did and why:

> **For he clave** (held fast) **to the Lord, and departed not from following him, but kept his commandments, which the Lord commanded Moses. And the Lord was with him; and he prospered whithersoever he went forth. . . .**
>
> **2 Kings 18:6,7**

Standing squarely on the "Jerusalem Place," Hezekiah shows us that trusting God and obeying God are for our good as well as for God's glory. His past can be our future. Prosperity follows keeping the Lord's commandments.

The story of Hezekiah as told in 2 Chronicles shows us more of his efforts to overhaul Judah's spiritual life as well as its political scene. He cleansed the temple from his father's evil practices, then rededicated it through the right sacrifices and with true worship. (2 Chronicles 29.)

As a Christian, do you want to be a Hezekiah or an Ahaz? Both were of the people of God, but one was faithful and obedient while the other opened the door to the world, the flesh, and the devil.

How many Christians live at the "place of Jerusalem" or are en route there, and how many live in Samaria, the place of compromise, sin, and rebellion?

However, "prosperity" because of trusting God and obedience does not mean nothing bad will ever happen to you. Jesus said He would be with us *through* trials, not keep us from them. He experienced trials and temptations, so why shouldn't we?

When the devil wanted to "sift Peter like wheat," Jesus did not protect him from the trial but prayed that Peter would have the strength to withstand the enemy. (Luke 22:31,32.)

So the time came when Hezekiah was tested.

The Dilemma of Hezekiah

After years of serving God and restoring the nation of Judah to the true worship of Jehovah, suddenly here comes God's man saying, "It's time for you to leave this life, Hezekiah."

What a rude awakening that must have been! Here he has done everything God has told him to do, here he is standing firmly in the "place of Jerusalem," and God is calling him home just when it looks as if he could have a great life.

In those days was Hezekiah sick unto death. And the prophet Isaiah the son of Amoz came to him, and said unto him, Thus saith the Lord, Set thine house in order; for thou shalt die, and not live.

2 Kings 20:1

He is now faced with wondering whether God is fair. Even the most spiritual of us will have to admit that some things God says we do not understand. There are some things we may not think are fair, some things may even make us a little angry, at least.

In these situations, you can sit down and "cry the blues" and have a pity party, you can actually turn bitter at God, you can accept the situation as is, or you can pray to God to see if something can be changed.

However, Hezekiah apparently understood that self-pity would leave him powerless to change things. He also knew better than to become bitter at God, because you cannot function in a right way in life if you harbor anything in you that is not like God.

Bitterness and unforgiveness are not worth what they will cost you in spiritual or in natural matters.

He did not try to blame Sister or Brother So-and-so. He did not play the "what-if" game, but he examined himself, his actions and his motives. Then he turned his face to the wall and began to talk to God:

I beseech thee, O Lord, remember now how I have walked before thee in truth and with a perfect heart, and have done that which is good in thy sight. And Hezekiah wept sore.

2 Kings 20:3

Notice that what he said to God was not spoken in pride or in presumption but with an humble heart. Otherwise, God would not have heard his prayer. Perhaps this sickness unto death was a blessing in disguise because it kept him humble. It kept him from becoming prideful as his great-grandfather had become.

Hezekiah was brought to the place where he said, "God, I did everything You told me to do, but what do You want me to do now? I preached and restored worship of You. I rebelled against the enemy and threw off his yoke. Now what must I do?"

It seems that many of those in our pulpits have lost the consideration to go the last mile of the way for a soul. Many have fought and won major spiritual battles. However, if God shows them their churches or ministries are about to die, they do not get humble and ask what else they can do.

We have become so secure and so complacent in the fact of our "Christian" nation that we walk by folks who do not know anything about God without even thinking about their situations. They wait on our tables, clean our hotel rooms, wash our cars, and check out our groceries without ever knowing that we are Christian.

I know Hezekiah was a king, nevertheless, we can be like him. When he went before God, it was not as a king. He did not talk to God from his earthly throne. He did not approach God by virtue of his kingly position and title. He went to God as a man with a record in Heaven.

When you go into a hospital to pray for the sick, you do not lay your ordination papers or your baptismal certificate on them and say, "Be healed because I am an elder, or an evangelist, or a missionary."

Many of us preachers are so busy administrating and doing the work of the Lord that we miss the main commandment of Jesus: "Go tell all the world about Me." (Mark 16:15.) We miss speaking honestly and truthfully to God about our accomplishments and our shortcomings.

Here is a man who, like the prophet Elijah, has rebuked a people, reawakened them to the things of God, and restored the nation to where they can truly again be called "the people of God." Then right in the midst of restoration, just when everything should be going well, a sunshiny day has turned to darkness and storm.

Sincere Prayer Brings Answers

Hezekiah turned his face to the wall and beseeched God humbly to look at his record and let his life be prolonged.

In an unusual example for those times, he did not yell after Isaiah to talk to God for him. He got serious and talked to God himself. It does not take God a long time to answer a sincere prayer in most cases. (Daniel's situation in interceding for the nation was different: Daniel 10:12,13.)

Before Isaiah could get out of the courtyard of the palace, God sent him back to Hezekiah. God told him what to do to heal the boil that apparently was infected or into blood poisoning and would have resulted in the king's death. (2 Kings 20:7.)

Notice that God did not do a miracle but used natural medicine to bring about the healing. In addition, he gave Hezekiah a specific number of years more to live and promised victory over Assyria, whose troops had conquered Israel not long before and carried off the Israelites of the ten and a half tribes.

> **Turn again, and tell Hezekiah . . . I have heard thy prayer, I have seen thy tears: behold, I will heal thee: on the third day thou shalt go up unto the house of the Lord. And I will add unto thy days fifteen years; and I will deliver thee and this city out of the hand of the king of Assyria . . . for mine own sake and for my servant David's sake.**
>
> **2 Kings 20:5,6**

Do you know that if Hezekiah had not prayed, he would have died?

God is saying today that, unless His people pray, we will perish. We will become past history, a great "mausoleum" instead of a living Church. This nation also will continue its downward slide to paganism. It seems this generation of the Church has forgotten how to pray earnestly and without ceasing.

Hezekiah had torn down the groves where worship was offered to Satan in the guise of idols and restored true worship of God.

We need national leaders today like this king of the past who can bring restoration into our future.

We need Church leaders who will "take the boards" off church doors and once again restore them as true houses of worship.

We need spiritual leaders not afraid to use the word "rebuke," not afraid to lose members, lose tithes, and lose honor in the world in order to tear down "shrines" to other gods.

Those shrines can be in people's lives or in local churches, as well as in the Church as a whole and in the nation. It seems that we are living in a strange hour, a time of great deception in the middle of great access to the truth.

[1]*Zondervan's NIV Bible Commentary*, Vol. I, p. 559.

9

A Place of Deception or Discernment

And Samuel spake unto all the house of Israel, saying, If ye do return unto the Lord with all your hearts, then put away the strange gods . . . from among you, and prepare your hearts unto the Lord, and serve him only: and he will deliver you out of the hand of the Philistines.

1 Samuel 7:3

This is an hour which our devout forefathers in this country would think was a horrible time in which to live. The Bible warned of a time like this when men would be lovers of themselves with a form of godliness that denied the power thereof. (2 Timothy 3:5.)

The Bible warned of seducing spirits who would pull off the "very elect" of God if it were possible. (2 Timothy 3:13; Mark 13:22.)

This seems to be such a time. Things of the flesh are predominant, truth and morality are obscured, and sin is not only accepted but acceptable. Even many Christians have been "brainwashed" by secular education systems that deny the existence of God and promote the preeminence of man.

In spite of all this, God has a remnant — individuals who have been chosen from their mothers' wombs to declare that, no matter what they see or experience, nothing matters but God..

They know life is not about how well they can do things, how talented they are, or what spiritual gifts operate through them.

They "know that they know" that living this life victoriously is all about God.

In this strange hour, God's true people should be "turning our faces to the wall" and seeking God to extend the life of the one country in the modern world that was founded on Him. We should be asking God for "a fig poultice" of His Spirit to heal the "boils" of sin and corruption that are killing our society.

Instead, too many of us are listening to seducing spirits.

"Seducing spirits" are demons who make the things of the world look so enticing that people are seduced into sin. The psychic hotlines are promoted by seducing spirits pulling on people to become involved in occult spiritual sins and bondage.

Let us again look at the history of Israel to gain insight into living in these strange times. One place in the Promised Land is mentioned several times as an important site for national affairs. That is *Mizpeh.* The original meaning is "watchtower, or place of watching."[1]

That means it was on a high hill overlooking surrounding territory. However, those "high places" also became the locations of shrines to idols that for centuries various kings of Judah either allowed to remain or followed God and pulled down.

Somehow, however, all of them never were eradicated or were rebuilt in more lax times. In other words, *Mizpeh* also sometimes was "a place of deception" as well as a watchtower.

When I was speaking once in the Los Angeles area, God gave me a word for the people there. He said:

"I understand the reason you are struggling so. It is because of the region, the area, you are inhabiting. You think it is a wonderful place to live because it is on the top of hills. You are living on "high places."

God went on to show me, however, that every place has a demonic spirit assigned to influence and seduce the people away from Him. If the demonic influence does not literally engulf individuals, it discourages or tries to defeat God's remnant.

Wherever you live or move, it would be wise to seek God in prayer as to what seducing spirit will be coming against you there. Demons assigned to Los Angeles are different than those assigned to Atlanta, for example. Spirits assigned to Atlanta are different from those over New York.

I was riding once through a large city when I saw a strong spirit, standing tall. At first, I thought perhaps it was an angel of the Lord appearing to give me an assignment. He had his arms folded and stood looking over the city.

I began to question in my mind, "Lord, what is that spirit?"

The Lord said, "That is the demon assigned to this city. If you are going to be successful here for Me, tackle that demon. He is the one who disperses the imps. He is the one over the incognito demons, the ones who live undercover."

Then He said to me, "Nathan, study Mizpeh. It is not a place for sinners, but a place designed for those who have a real walk with Me. Unsaved people have never been to Mizpeh. Those who have never had hope in Me or a walk with Me cannot go there.

I said, "Why is that, God?"

He answered, "That is because of what Mizpeh represents."

The Counterfeit Mizpeh

However, there is a "Mizpeh" that is counterfeit, a place of deception where the high places of God have been infiltrated and perverted into demonic high places.

The real Mizpeh is a place of discernment, a place where you can look out over the surrounding territories and see enemies coming.

The counterfeit Mizpeh is a place of deception where everything looks like gold, silver, or diamonds — but is brass and rotting wood underneath..

If you have a real hope in God, if you have planted your feet solidly on the Rock Christ Jesus, if you have your foundation in "Jerusalem," you can discern true from false, counterfeit from real.

Someone without God or someone who has not been through the "Jerusalem place" will look at the same territory and be deceived. His or her eyes will be dazzled by fake spirituality or the enticements of the world, the flesh, and the devil.

One of the saddest things in the world to me is to see a saint of God in Mizpeh who thinks something is right when it is wrong. Everything sounds all right, everything looks good, but in my spirit, there is an unsettled feeling, a witness that everything really is all wrong.

The place called Mizpeh in Scripture was a place where the Israelites were gathered several times on matters of national importance. One time before Israel was a nation with kings, the prophet Samuel gathered the people to Mizpeh to repent of idolatry and pull down the "strange" (foreign) gods.

At that point, the strongest enemy of the Israelites was the Philistines. When they heard that great numbers of Israelites were gathered on Mizpeh repenting, fasting, and praying, the Philistines "drew near" to battle against them.

This was during the 20-year period when the ark of the covenant had been captured and was held by the Philistines. Yet Samuel told the people that if they returned to the Lord with all their hearts, He would give them victory over their enemy. (1 Samuel 7:3.)

The spirits over the Philistines (actually over the entire land of Canaan) did not have to be spiritually discerned. They were baals (various gods) and Ashtaroth, whose images were to be found all over the land, particularly on the high places.

Anytime in their history that the Israelites did not have strong godly leadership, they tended to slip into idol worship, into going after "strange" gods, those foreign to the followers of Jehovah.

Without prophets, priests, or kings to keep them focused on God, Israel would become unsatisfied with the God of their past deliverance, the God of their fathers, and the God of their covenant. They would develop "itching ears" and run after something they could see with their natural eyes. (2 Timothy 4:3.)

That sounds like our society, does it not? God told me our problem today is that we are dealing with people who do not have a sense of real spirituality. There is a great spiritual hunger today, but many are running to counterfeit Mizpehs, to foreign gods, and to strange doctrines.

Notice that the Philistines really came after the Israelites when they began to repent. When they decided to rededicate their lives to the God of Abraham, Isaac, and Jacob is when the devil began to come against them.

One of the biggest deceptions sometimes told to unbelievers is that, once you come to God, you will have no more trouble! Actually, when you come to God, your eternal security is settled, but in this life, that is usually the beginning of trouble.

Just let a person get saved or a backslidden person return to God, and the same friends who smiled with him, laughed with him, or joked with him, instantaneously turn and come against him. That newly saved or newly restored person can feel as if he or she is a tiny minority.

That is the position the Israelites repenting at Mizpeh were in: few compared to the armies of their enemy. However, even one believer aligned with God constitutes a majority.

God and You Make a Majority

The Israelites gathered at Mizpeh showed that their priorities were finally in order, at least for that time and in that place. They begged Samuel not to quit crying out to God to save them from the Philistines.

So Samuel made a sacrifice and cried unto the Lord for Israel, and the Lord heard him. A footnote in one *King James Version* of the Bible says that the Lord *answered* him.[2] (1 Samuel 7:9.)

There is something about making a sacrifice to God that He honors. Some say the greater the sacrifice, the greater the blessing. At any rate, the Israelites won a great battle that day but only with God's help.

> **. . . The Lord thundered with a great thunder on that day upon the Philistines, and discomfited them; and they were smitten before Israel. And the men of Israel went out of Mizpeh, and pursued the Philistines, and smote them, until they came under Beth-car.**
>
> **1 Samuel 7:10,11**

Mizpeh is the best place to come out of and take the might of God against the enemy. On the "watchtower" in the spirit, you can perceive the enemy coming and not only intercede but make a sacrifice if the attack looks great. Then when you are firmly and securely on God's side, you can be sure He will "thunder a great thunder" on your behalf.

The important thing is not whether God is on your side, but whether you are on His side.

After the battle, Samuel set up a stone, a monument to God, and named it *Ebenezer*, or "Hitherto hath the Lord helped us." The word *ebenezer* literally means "stone of help."[3]

Jesus is the Stone, or Rock, of our salvation. He is our ever-present help in time of trouble. God was the Stone for the Israelites.

So the Philistines were subdued, and they came no more into the coast of Israel: and the hand of the Lord was against the Philistines all the days of Samuel. And the cities which the Philistines had taken from Israel were restored . . . And there was peace between Israel and the Amorites.

1 Samuel 7:13,14

Talk about the importance of mounting a watch for God and against the enemy! If the Church as a whole would repent, tear down false gods and deceptive ideas and doctrines, and make a sacrifice to God — fast and pray — our enemies of secularism, occultism, and complacency would "come near our coasts no more.”."

Obviously the key is prayer. We need prayer from intercessors, prayer from leaders, and the corporate prayer of agreement among believers. Our enemies are many compared to the remnant of true believers. However, if we get totally over on God's side, we will have a majority.

Prayer brings results. If we are praying, and there are no results, something is not wrong with God. Something is wrong with us. He said He would hear us before we call. (Matthew 6:8.)

From my childhood, I saw the results of prayer in my mother's life. Sometimes we would be hungry. I remember her putting a big pot on the stove. She would put some fatback in there and some water. Then she would set the table — plate, bowl, saucer, cup, napkin, knife, fork, spoon, and two glasses on the side.

Time and time again, I remember her doing this and then saying, "Now, you all go and play." Then she would begin to pray.

"Lord, if You do not do it for me, do it for my babies. Give my babies a meal. Help them now in the name of Jesus. I do not know how You are going to do it, but You have never failed me yet.

"Lord, if You do not provide for them, they will be pulled off into maybe selling drugs. They will not stay in school and go to college. They will not get jobs and try to help me and one another."

She would stay on her knees until there was a knock at the door. It might be a neighbor with bags of groceries, but it would be something.

A neighbor might say, "I hope you don't mind, but we came into some extra money. I was in the store when something said to pick up a few things for you."

Out would come steak or hamburger, bread, and cans of corn or something. Then we would eat!

My mother did not know to call God *Ebenezer*, but she was actually saying:

"God, You can do it. You are Ebenezer, the God who can help and will help, the God who has helped me in times past."

I grew up in one of those churches where we had some strong mothers. They always dressed in black or white with maybe a little blue or brown in there. They put little collars on their dresses and always wore something on their heads and carried big Bibles.

Whenever they saw you, they would say, "Praise the Lord, son. Oh, I was praying for you. The Lord bless you." And they would give you a great big bear hug.

In those churches and those homes with praying mothers, we learned that real prayer brings results.

[1]*New Bible Dictionary*, p. 785.

[2]Footnote to 1 Samuel 7:12 in *The Holy Bible, King James Version*, (Nashville: Thomas Nelson Publishers, 1994), Giant Print Center-Column Reference Edition, p. 418.

[3]Ibid.

10

How To Bring Back the Ark

And David said unto all the congregation of Israel, If it seem good unto you, and that it be of the Lord our God, let us . . . bring again the ark of our God to us: for we enquired not at it in the days of Saul.

1 Chronicles 13:2,3

Samuel was a "circuit riding" prophet and judge. He traveled from Gilgal to Bethel to Mizpeh and around again, from "circling the wagons" to religious freedom and/or sometimes religiosity, and back to the high places. (1 Samuel 7:16.) He fought the deception of other gods outside of Israel and of pride and self-righteousness in Israel.

Then Samuel got old, which happens to all of us who live long enough. However, the old wise prophet made a mistake. He did not mentor someone to come after him. He was permissive and apparently did not discipline his own sons, although he established them as judges.

He did not hold his own children to his godly standards or to the standards to which he tried to hold the Israelites. His sons became corrupt, took bribes, perverted judgment, and did not walk in his ways. (1 Samuel 8:1-3.)

At that point, the Israelites forgot that it was Samuel on the high hill praying and sacrificing for them while the Lord defeated the Philistines. They began to think it was their own might. They began to think their big problem was not turning away from God. They thought it was not having a king like other nations.

They began to want to be like the tribes and nations around them and said to Samuel **. . . make us a king to judge us like all the nations** (1 Samuel 8:5).

Samuel warned them at the command of God about the danger of totalitarian power, of military conscription and taxes, and of the oppression that could come from kingship. (1 Samuel 8:10-18.) However, they refused to listen:

> **. . . Nay; but we will have a king over us; that we also may be like all the nations; and that our king may judge us, and go out before us, and fight our battles.**
>
> **1 Samuel 8:19,20**

Then God said, "Samuel, they are not rejecting you, but Me. They are rejecting My rule over them in favor of a man's rule."

That was when Israel became a nation like other nations, no longer directly under God through judges and prophets who were chosen by God and who spoke for Him. Only a few kings throughout the history of Israel and Judah truly spoke for God and ruled for Him after that.

So Israel got a king like the other nations but it was still many years before God's presence was officially in the nation again. It was years before the ark of the covenant was returned to Israel. David, who was the second king and truly God's man, had to learn how "to bring back the ark."

That is what we need today: Some Davids who will learn how to bring back the ark to the nation.

The ark of the covenant was made according to specific instructions God gave Moses on Mount Sinai. (Exodus 25:8-22.) This chest overlaid with pure gold inside and out was to be a *sanctuary,* a "dwelling place" for God among the Israelites.

The ark was constructed with a "mercy seat" on its top between the replicas of two cherubim, and the presence of God descended there.

And there I will meet with thee, and I will commune (speak) **with thee from above the mercy seat. . . .**

Exodus 25:22

In the ark were placed items to remind Israel of God's love and justice. There was Aaron's rod that budded during the confrontation with Pharaoh, the stone tablets on which God wrote the Ten Commandments, and a golden jar of manna from the wilderness years. (Hebrews 9:4.)

The items in the ark represented God's supernatural power and protection, God's Word, and God's provision.

Our Hearts Are "Arks"

The ark was a visible symbol of God's promise to dwell with them as "a holy people." It was proof that He was with them. However, they began to look on it as a talisman, a charm, and not just symbolic of the presence of God. They began to think it had power in itself.

Possibly they would have come to worship it instead of God if it had not disappeared from sight about the time of the Babylonian exile of Judah. In the days of Samuel, Saul, and David, however, the Israelites failed to see that, even when the ark was not present, they still had the protection of God. The key to His help and protection was to truly repent and genuinely follow Him.

Today, the "ark" of the New Covenant is the heart of a believer. The Apostle Paul wrote that our bodies are "temples" where God dwells. (1 Corinthians 6:19.) The ark of the Old Covenant was situated in the "Holy of Holies" of the tabernacle and, later the temple. It was located in the very heart of God's house.

Church buildings are not God's houses, but places where "God's houses" meet. Every Christian is a "temple," a "house" wherein God dwells, and in each heart are the "testimonies" of God's actions on our behalf and a record of our worship of Him.

In our hearts should be witnesses of God's power and protection, His Word, and evidence of His provision for us in all areas of life. Too many believers today do not have those things in their "arks." Instead, they are relying on the economy, on the government, and on their own efforts.

Israel's first king, which they had demanded of Samuel, was Saul, a Benjamite, who began well but ended badly. He came to rely on his own efforts. From a humble, personable young man, standing head and shoulders above most other Israelites (1 Samuel 10:23), he fell into pride, rebellion, and witchcraft. (1 Samuel 15:23.)

Saul died in disgrace and lost the right for his sons to continue on the throne of Israel. When he was given a command to obey God, he chose to disobey. (1 Samuel 15:22.) Then after he was rebuked by Samuel, instead of repenting, he was more concerned with his reputation among his peers. (1 Samuel 15:30.)

Succeeding Saul was David, who followed after God's heart all his life in spite of falling into grievous sins. David, however, never got into pride and never stopped truly worshipping God. He was quick to receive correction and rebuke and quick to repent. (2 Samuel 12:13.)

After David was received as king by all Israel and had defeated enemies on all sides, one day he decided it was time to go get the ark. It had been at Kirjathjearim in the territory of Judah since being carried off by the Philistines. (1 Samuel 7:1,2.)

Saul would not have necessarily been replaced because he made a mistake or even because he sinned – David was not. God does not kill you for everything you do wrong. He loves you in spite of your wrongdoing.

Saul was replaced because, instead of acknowledging his sin and repenting of rebellion and disobedience, he covered his sin.

None of us is able to live, think, and act absolutely perfectly. We are being "perfected" every day that we allow the Holy Spirit to change us. The thing that gains us God's favor, next to obedience, is quickly confessing mistakes and sins and repenting. (1 John 1:9.)

The thing that is outstanding about David is that he began humble and stayed humble. He was out in the fields minding his own business when Samuel came to anoint him. He was the youngest son, whose brothers apparently rode roughshod over him. (1 Samuel 16:11, 17:28,29.) Perhaps that taught him humility!

After he was anointed, he did not change but went on doing what he was assigned to do. He was not like some people now who prophesy one time and then call themselves prophets or who preach one good inspired message and want to take over pastorates.

We do not have enough individuals selling out to God today. From Mizpeh, the enemy is overrunning us. Who is praying on the mountain today while the soldiers of God fight? When was the last time you went on a fast not called by your pastor?

When was the last time your church called an all-night prayer meeting? This time of strange gods and doctrines is too crucial for us to stumble over things of the flesh. We are dealing with demons that come out only by fasting and prayer. (Matthew 17:21.)

Flesh stinks in the nostrils of God. Every true Christian needs to recognize that wherever he or she is placed by God is strategically in line with His purposes. We are to witness to those we meet about Jesus, to cast out devils, preach salvation, and healing to the sick in mind and body.

We Need To Become of One Mind

The first thing David did when he thought of bringing the ark back to Israel was gather the people together. Some things cannot be accomplished without unity of minds and goals.

When the Holy Spirit was sent to earth to inhabit God's people, it was to a group praying together in one mind and one spirit, which means one aim, one purpose, and one heart. (Acts 2:1.)

The devil knows that too, which is why he encouraged the generation right after the flood to remain in one place and unite in a plan to build a tower that would reach to Heaven.

> **And the whole earth was of one language, and of one speech . . . let us make us a name, lest we be scattered abroad upon the face of the whole earth.**
>
> **Genesis 11:1,4**

Knowing what can be accomplished by people thinking and acting together, God came to earth and scattered the people at Babel. (Genesis 11:6-9.) They had set out to build a tower to Heaven in rebellion to God's command to multiply across the earth. (Genesis 1:28, 9:7.)

So David knew the return of the ark could not be accomplished without the people being of one mind and heart in "solemn assembly."

> **So David gathered all Israel together, from Shihor of Egypt even unto the entering of Hemath, to bring the ark of God from Kirjathjearim.**
>
> **1 Chronicles 13:5**

David gathered not only the leaders, the Levites, and the men, but everyone who would come. He gathered them from the north, south, east, and west. He pointed out that during the whole reign of Saul, Israel had not been able to enquire of God at the ark or repent at the mercy seat.

The ark represented the presence of God in the nation. It was to remind them of God. Is there something in your life that makes you remember God? Can you say because this or that happened to me, I am where I am today, and if God had not been present, I would not be here?

It might be a physical healing. It might have been an accident or a potential death of a loved one that was turned by God from disaster to good. Whatever it was, have you now forgotten the importance of the presence of God in your life? Is your "ark" sitting on the sidelines in some other place?

Remember that the things in the ark represent what should be in our hearts:

1. The tablets on which God wrote the Ten Commandments with His own finger represent His Word in our lives. Without His Word we would have no truth, no guidance, and no promise of the future. David declared His Word a light to his feet and to his pathway and said it was hidden in his heart. (Psalm 119:105.)

Where there is no Word, there is no conception of God, because **in the beginning was the Word, and the Word was with God, and the Word *was* God** (John 1:1.)

2. Secondly, the golden pot of manna reminds us that *God is our Source.* The Israelites were fed in the wilderness years when there was no food. We also can learn from the manna that God gives us what we need, He does not pander to the lusts of the flesh. (Numbers 11:4,5.)

Israel got into trouble once on the wilderness trek at Kibrothhattaavah (the place where those who lusted after flesh were buried, or "graves of craving" – Numbers 11:34).

God said to me once, "Nathan, long before Paul was able to write, **My God shall supply all of my needs according to His riches in glory,** Moses was able to write *Jehovah Jireh, the Lord who is my provider.* (Philippians 4:19.)

In addition to food and water, God kept their shoes and clothes from wearing out during the 40-year sojourn. (Deuteronomy 29:5.) Notice that He did not create new ones for them each time they wanted a change or got tired of the same old fashions!

3. Then we come to Aaron's rod, which was the object of God's supernatural power. However, the rod had other meanings.

It was a branch of the almond tree, a tree that brings forth nuts that are good for the health. Medical reports say that eating half a dozen almonds a day helps prevent heart attacks.

When I looked at a picture of Aaron's rod and the almond tree, I said, "God, what are You telling me?"

He said, "Nathan Simmons, what the tree brings forth is nuts, which must be crushed, chopped, cut in half, or squeezed to extract the oil. Oil represents the anointing."

There are some things you have to go through to get to the anointing. We cannot base our relationship or our position in God on how we feel. If we were not such "hard nuts," it would not require squeezing or cracking us open to get the anointing, to get to the oil of the Spirit.

Therefore, from David's experience, we can see that "bringing back the ark" required hiding God's Word in our hearts, looking only to Him for all our needs, and being put through God's oil press to extract the precious anointing. "Bringing back the ark" means tarrying at the mercy seat in repentance until God says to move.

Israel, from the last days of Samuel until David stabilized the nation, was in a time of transition. Usually, in the natural as well as in spiritual maturity, things do not happen all of a sudden although it may look like that on the surface.

If you have discernment, you can get a glimpse of what is happening. If not, you can look back after the fact and see that things were leading up to change in individuals or in groups. You can see that developments were in progress that led from one place to another.

At this time in Church history, we also are in a transition period. Will things lead to a better place or will we lose ground? That depends on our attitudes, our obedience to God, and our actions in the next few years.

11

A Place of Transition

So David brought not the ark home to himself . . . but carried it aside. . . . And the ark of God remained with the family of Obed-edom in his house three months. And the Lord blessed the house of Obed-edom, and all that he had.

1 Chronicles 13:13,14

Kirjath-jearim, the place where the ark stayed for those years, means "the city of forests."[1] It was a place of transition, perhaps a place where Israel could not see the forest for the trees, which often happens during transitional times.

Places of transition are extremely important. They determine whether we, the Church, nations, or the world go on to the next higher spiritual place. Wrong choices, wrong actions, missing God by doing your own thing costs you progress and causes you to stagnate where you are or slide backwards.

It is crucial that we restore the "ark" to the Church, the collective Temple of God today.

It is crucial that we return to seeking God at the "mercy seat," whether that is church altars, private prayer rooms, or simply spending time on our knees.

The literal "mercy seat" for the Israelites was centered on the ark between statues of two cherubim depicted on their knees and in a worship mode. The angelic beings were to be examples of how the Israelite priests were to seek God on behalf of the people.

Angelic beings worship God in Heaven day in and day out. They do not have as much to worship Him over as we do, yet they worship. They were never fallen beings whom God sent His only Son to redeem.

Apparently, not being a race but created individually, angelic beings had no right to choose to be anything but what they were created. Therefore, there was no redemption possible for those who fell with Satan, no way to send another Head of Race to pay the penalty for all born of Adam, the first head of race.

Redemption would have to have been provided separately for each one. A perfect being would have to have died for each angelic being, not through a covenant extending to all born of a head of race. For this reason, the children of God will sing a song the angels cannot sing.

How much more should we be willing and ready to worship God than those who kept their first estate and never needed redeeming?

When we read the account of the restoration of the ark to Israel, we can see that the first attempt was a disaster. David and the people had good intentions *but they did not have proper knowledge*.

A man named Uzza had good intentions as he reached to steady the ark when the oxen stumbled while pulling it on a cart. However, he died instantly, because no unsanctified person can touch the presence of God and live.

Good Intentions Will Not Replace Knowledge

God had warned Moses about how to handle the ark (Numbers 4:5,15), but David's group of well-intentioned people dancing and singing before the Lord had a lack of knowledge. In later years, God told the prophet Hosea that His people were being destroyed for lack of knowledge. (Hosea 4:6.)

Today, we are in the same situation. Many churchgoing Christians, who say they have been born again, have little knowledge of God's Word. Most depend on anything but God to meet their needs, and would be highly indignant at the idea they might be hardened enough to need "crushing."

Thousands of people who call themselves Christian are being destroyed for lack of knowledge of God's Word, His will, and His ways.

David had to back up and start over. He did what he should have in the beginning. Somehow, perhaps by consulting the priests and Levites, he found out God's instructions for handling the ark.

Why was Obed-edom blessed while the ark was in his home? When we check out his ancestry, we find he *was* a Levite of the tribe set aside by God to take care of the ark and the sacred items in the tabernacle (the tent of worship carried through the wilderness and used until Solomon built the temple).

He was of the clan of Kohath, the family of Korah, and a Korahite gatekeeper. He also was a musician, and he met the requirements for a caretaker of the ark. (1 Chronicles 26:1-4, 15:18,21,24.)

In addition to the people specified by God to carry the ark, it was to have been transported by hand, not on a cart. Even by authorized carriers, it was not to be touched "lest they die." (Numbers 4:15.)

Do we have Christians today, even preachers, who touch the glory? Do we decide for ourselves how to "transport" the ark? Do we have those who "handle" the things of God with unclean hands?

The first thing David had the people do when he went after the ark a second time *was to have them sanctify themselves*. He brought them together again in unity, then he went on to sanctification (cleansing) and preparation, as well as appointing those whom God had designated. (1 Chronicles 4-11.)

> **. . . Sanctify yourselves, both ye and your brethren, that ye may bring up the ark of the Lord God of Israel. . . . For because ye did it not at the first, the Lord our God made a breach upon us, for that we sought him not after the due order.**
>
> **1 Chronicles 15:12,13**

The group bringing back the ark now put on the right clothing, not just any old everyday clothes, but those representing righteousness. Every piece of clothing designated for the priests and Levites to wear had a symbolic significance.

Transitional times tend to be chaotic, unorganized, and characterized by immorality and license to sin. Guidelines have gone by the wayside, patterns of society blur, and the economy becomes unstable.

Some of those times in our fairly recent history have been Reconstruction after the Civil War, the Roaring Twenties and Depressed Thirties, and the rebellious Sixties. After those times, American culture changed, politics changed, and people changed.

In this time of the late 90s and early 21st century, however, we have denounced God, which did not happen in any of those earlier transitional times in this country. The Bible declares that a country which denounces their God will find themselves on their way down.

France denounced God in its transitional time of the late 1700s and became an atheistic nation easily conquered by Germany in both world wars.

> **Righteousness exalteth a nation: but sin is a reproach to any people.**
>
> **Proverbs 14:34**

The place of transition always is a place where nuts are crushed and either thrown away or the oil extracted. We can look at individuals today who are anointed and not see the price that had to be paid for that.

Sometimes, in order for people to move in the anointing, their feelings have to be hurt. They have to experience rejection and even be despised and realize that none of that matters. When you have God, what do your hurt feelings matter?

Instead of a crushing time to bring forth anointing, our churches are mostly living in "Bethel," where the religious spirit is producing replications of traditional ways of doing things. The "ways of the fathers" are more followed than the ways of God.

God does not want us to just "go through the motions" of "the way we do it in this church." He does not want new converts to be "programmed" according to the traditions of a particular church or denomination.

There must be a reality in God, a place where people dare to be different if that is what it takes. Samuel became a different kind of prophet than the priest Eli, because Samuel started in God at an early age and did things God's way. (1 Samuel 3:19,20.)

When Samuel was a child, the Bible says it was a very dark time in Israel. There was "no open vision" and the Word of God was very rare in those days. (1 Samuel 3:1.) Yet this one person grew up to make a real difference in Israel.

I go here and go there, and the thing that grieves me about this day is that we have mega ministries, but we are not turning out the quality of saints anointed for this time. The sheep are famished for the true and vital Word of God, and are being fed on dried up grass.

The messages coming forth now are not of repentance and change of heart, but are lopsided and unbalanced. Even in Spirit-filled churches and denominations, we hear prosperity, we hear psychology, we even hear politics and social issues, but few messages that penetrate the heart.

Why does it matter if we come through the times of transition to be like Samuel and make a difference? It matters because, if we individually or as a nation have matured through the various places on our spiritual journeys, we get to the place where God fights the battles.

Over and over in the history of Israel and Judah, we find those times when they wholeheartedly followed God, and He would say "the battle is Mine."

Of course, the Israelites had to fight, but God turned things so that they won against great odds. Sometimes, He did things supernaturally to their enemies and they did not have to actually fight. Then sometimes He simply empowered them to win.

Let's back up in time again to more than 150 years before King Hezekiah of Judah when Solomon's great-great grandson Jehoshaphat ruled Judah. This was the era when Ahab ruled Israel, and Elijah was just beginning his ministry.

Jehoshaphat was one of the most devout and prosperous kings of Judah, the best to rule since his forefather Solomon. His life is an example of how one should live to be in a position for God to fight one's battles.

[1]*New Bible Dictionary,* p. 665.

12

A Place Where God Fights the Battle

And he said, Hearken ye, all Judah, and ye inhabitants of Jerusalem, and thou king Jehoshaphat, Thus saith the Lord unto you, Be not afraid nor dismayed by reason of this great multitude; for the battle is not yours, but God's.

2 Chronicles 20:15

During this time of transition, I believe God is moving on His people to put their priorities in order. I am convinced He is no longer going to "play second fiddle" to foreign gods, strange doctrines, and things of the flesh in His people.

He wants the Body of Christ to know that whatever the trial, the test, the tribulation, the temptation, the sickness or financial problems, or even the depravity of the culture around us, *He is the true and living God.* With Him, all things *are* possible. (Matthew 19:26.)

Sometimes it takes hard times, times when things are shaking around us, to bring us to the place of totally aligning ourselves on God's side. At these times, it seems God sits high and looks low and shakes His head at what is going on in the world.

The Bible says that He looked on the earth at the time of the flood and actually "came down" at the time of the Tower of Babel to see firsthand what was going on. (Genesis 6:12, 11:5.) Later, the Lord told Abraham that He would "go down" to Sodom and Gomorrah and see if it was as bad there as the cry of it that had come up to Him. (Genesis 18:20,21.)

Through His Holy Spirit's presence in the Body of Christ since Jesus ascended to Heaven, He *is* here all the time looking around at what is going on. In Jehoshaphat's time, God had Elijah in Israel and other seers in Judah keeping an eye on events and speaking forth God's Word to the kings.

Jehoshaphat had a tragic example in his father, Asa, so perhaps that caused him to seek God, walk in God's commandments and the ways of David, and not follow the pattern of corrupt Israel. (2 Chronicles 17:3,4.) Therefore, the Bible says:

> **. . . The Lord stablished the kingdom in his hand; and all Judah brought to Jehoshaphat presents; and he had riches and honour in abundance. And his heart was lifted up in the ways of the Lord: moreover he took away the high places and groves out of Judah.**
>
> **2 Chronicles 17:5,6**

Judah in King Asa's day was attacked by Israel under a king who moved in on Judah's territory and blocked the people from leaving or entering the nation. Instead of repenting and looking to God for protection, Asa gave bribes to the king of Syria asking him to attack Israel and pull them away from Judah.

Syria did, but God sent the seer Hanani to warn Asa that Syria would turn on him because he had relied on man and not God. Did Asa repent? No, instead he went into a rage and threw the messenger in prison, oppressing some of the people at the same time. (2 Chronicles 16:7-10.)

It was not long until Asa developed a "great" disease in his feet but still did not seek God, so he died. Do you think that was an object lesson for his son Jehoshaphat? I do! He became an entirely different kind of king.

Jehoshaphat sent "princes" (elders in Judah), priests, and Levites to teach about God in all the cities of Judah. This resulted in the "fear of the Lord" falling on surrounding nations so they not only made no war against this king but even brought him tribute and gifts. (2 Chronicles 17:7-11.)

Jehoshaphat became increasingly powerful, built castles and storehouses, and much business and trade was being carried on. Also, many "mighty men of valor" were attracted to Jerusalem to enlist in his armies. (2 Chronicles 17:12-14.)

It is interesting that Jehoshaphat means "He who has been judged by God."[1] It is great to have been judged by God and not found wanting. When you know who you are in Christ, when you have a clear conscience, and when you know you are obedient and willing to do God's will, it takes away all insecurity.

As I studied these accounts, God showed me that the spiritual state of the kings made such a great difference to the fate of the nations because the enemy attacks the "head" first. Whatever you experience as an individual affects your head. If you hit your hand or stump your toe, your head will register the pain first.

That is why the Bible tells us to guard our minds, to fix our minds on Him, and to "pull down" any ideas, philosophy, or beliefs that would exalt itself against Him.

> **(For the weapons of our warfare are not carnal, but mighty through God to the pulling down of strong holds;)** ***casting down imaginations*** **and every high thing that exalteth itself against the knowledge of God, and bringing into captivity every thought to the obedience of Christ.**
>
> **2 Corinthians 10:4,5**

When your mind is set on God, Jesus truly is your Head, and God fights your battles, but a carnal mind will get you in trouble.

> **For to be carnally minded is death; but to be spiritually minded is life and peace. Because the carnal mind is enmity against God: for it is not subject to the law of God, neither indeed can be.**
>
> **Romans 8:6,7**

Carnally minded Christians have no security or peace and cannot obey God. You might say they are saints with split personalities.

Saints with Split Personalities

After Ahab became king, Judah and Israel became at peace again with one another. Jehoshaphat even allied himself by marriage with Ahab. (2 Chronicles 18:1.) However, he brought his attitude to God into his dealings with the king of Israel, especially at the strategic battle where God's judgment on Ahab was fulfilled.

Jehoshaphat was the one who refused to believe false prophets who predicted success for Ahab in his final battle with Syria. He asked for another prophet of the Lord of whom to enquire. However, when the prophet Micaiah was brought, Ahab refused to believe him and put him in prison on bread and water. (2 Chronicles 18:24-26.)

Like many of us today, when the prophet warned him of what was to come, Ahab accused the man of God of never telling him anything good but of prophesying evil for him. Any more than Ahab, most of us do not want to hear warnings, but "thus saith the Lord, you will prosper and be in good health."

Ahab persuaded Jehoshaphat to pretend to be him in an effort to avoid the fulfillment of prophecy. However, the Syrians saw through the ruse, saving the king of Judah. (2 Chronicles 18:29-31.)

Ahab was shot not on purpose by Syrian soldiers but by a "random" arrow that "accidentally" struck his armor just at the right place to kill him. (2 Chronicles 18:32-34.) When God pronounces a true prophetic word, it cannot be avoided.

Sometime after Jehoshaphat returned safely and in peace to Jerusalem, there came a time when Judah truly needed God to fight for them. Those attacking Judah were of Moab and Ammon, descendants of Lot, the nephew of Abraham, and far-removed cousins of the Israelites.

They were out of place relationship-wise and out of place geographically when they came against Judah. The Moabites and

Ammonites were wealthy people who usually lived in mountainous areas.

I wondered why they came against Jehoshaphat, whose first act upon hearing of the multitudes massing against him, was *to seek the Lord* and proclaim a fast.

I wondered how the Moabites could be so warlike against distant relatives, and yet some of them were kind and followed God, such as Ruth, David's ancestress. (See the book of Ruth.)

The Lord said to me, "Nathan, their wealth was known throughout all of the lands around, but these people had split personalities."

I compared what we know about those two peoples with what we can see about the saints of God today, and I saw that we have many who apparently have split personalities.

Sometimes you see them, they are happy; sometimes they are sad — or mad. One minute they are shouting and praying in the spirit, then the next week they are wondering if God is really who He says He is.

The "split" comes between the soul and spirit. Whatever is in your mind, will, and emotions that has not been submitted to your spirit under God will come out sooner or later.

You can hide it, tuck wrong attitudes away nice and neat, but if you are arrogant, if you are hard-hearted, if you are not submitted to God totally, it will not be long before those things show.

The founding fathers of these people were the product of incest between Lot and his daughters. (Genesis 19:30-38.) Moab and Ammon, the sons of these two unions, did not know whether to call Lot "father" or "grandfather." When people are mixed up in their minds, they will be envious and jealous of those who have peace and are secure in who they are.

Jealousy should cause you to feel pity for someone, because it is the outward manifestation of a struggle within their souls. When you do not know who you are, you will try to be everyone else. You will be envious of those who do know who they are.

When you know who you are in Christ, you will recognize that God sends rain on the just and unjust alike (Matthew 5:45), and that all things are in the hand of the Lord. In other words, you are not the center of the universe upon whom all things depend.

When the writer of Chronicles wrote that "Jehoshaphat feared," he did not mean fear as in fear of the dark, fear of his enemies, or fear of death. The Hebrew word *yare*, in this context, means "reverent."[2]

A Place of Prayer

Once again, we come to the point that, in time of trouble, the only place to be is in a *place of prayer*.

Jehoshaphat not only called a fast, but he began to "lay hold" of God, not out of fear but from faith and trust in God. His prayer, as he led the people of Judah gathered in Jerusalem, is a model of how to pray.

He reminded God of who He is and of His relationship with the people of Judah.

He reminded God (and himself) of what God had done in the past.

He reminded God of the treachery of Ammon and Moab against him in the past and spelled out what the two nations were now trying to do (as if God did not know). However, bringing things to God's remembrance also strengthens our faith and trust in Him.

> **. . . O Lord God of our fathers, art not thou God in heaven? and rulest not thou over all the kingdoms of the heathen? and in thine hand is there not power and might, so that none is able to withstand thee? Art not thou our God, who didst drive out the inhabitants of this land before thy**

people Israel, and gavest it to the seed of Abraham thy friend for ever?

2 Chronicles 20:6,7

As the king prayed, the Spirit of the Lord moved on one of the Levites in the middle of the congregation standing before Jehoshaphat. This man, Jahaziel, stood up and spoke a word from the Lord:

And he said, Hearken ye, all Judah, and ye inhabitants of Jerusalem, and thou king Jehoshaphat, Thus saith the Lord unto you, Be not afraid nor dismayed by reason of this great multitude; ***for the battle is not your's, but God's.***

2 Chronicles 20:15

Then the Lord through this little Levite gave them instructions for the battle, which way to go, and where to find the enemy. (2 Chronicles 20:16.) He said:

Ye shall not need to fight in this battle: set yourselves, stand ye still, and see the salvation of the Lord with you, O Judah and Jerusalem: fear not, nor be dismayed; to morrow go out against them: for the Lord will be with you.

2 Chronicles 20:17

Then everyone fell on their faces and worshipped God, ending the "service" by standing up again and praising God for all they were worth.

Next morning, they set off along the way God had said with assigned singers walking out front of the army praising the Lord. Guess what? When they got to the battlefield, all they could find were dead bodies. The enemy had killed one another.

In addition, it took the Judaites three days to gather up all the spoils, and they sang and praised God all the way back to Jerusalem. (2 Chronicles 20:22-28.)

How do you get to that place where God fights your battles?

You walk through Gilgal, Gilead, Bethel, Jericho, and the Jordan. You come down from Mizpeh into a valley, a place of transition, and get to the end of yourself. You finally realize that, in yourself, you can do nothing. (John 15:5.)

Then you fast and pray, worship and praise, and listen for God to tell you to "stand still" and let Him be God.

You must be careful, however, not to confuse enemy attacks with God giving you the hard thing for which you asked, the hard thing that will move you from one place to the next. You must not be surprised when God answers your prayer for a hard thing.

[1]*Smith's Bible Dictionary*, p. 283.

[2]*Strong's Concordance*, "Hebrew Dictionary," p. 59, #3373.

13

Don't Be Surprised When God Answers

And he said, The things which are impossible with men are possible with God.

Luke 18:27

Was Jehoshaphat surprised when the battle was over before they got there? When he asked God for a hard thing, and God answered, were the Judaites surprised?

No, they believed God, and it happened.

Was Elisha surprised when he got a double portion of Elisha's anointing? Certainly not. The sons of the prophets apparently were surprised, and so was the youth gang who taunted "old baldy," but not Elisha.

If you ask God for a hard thing, a thing that you desperately need, or something that will "crush" the nut that is you and release the anointing, do not be surprised. Surprise shows doubt. It shows that you really did not expect God to answer your prayer.

One minister tells of praying for a young man in one of his meetings who received a miracle. However, the minister was surprised. He began to marvel and say, "What about that?" He began to act as if he never expected God to move — and the boy lost his eyesight again.

The minister learned a hard lesson and never did that again. So if you get the hard thing for which you have asked, accept it with praise and thanksgiving.

Do not be like the woman the old saints tell about who read the verse about mountains moving if you believe. (Matthew 17:20.) She prayed before she went to bed one night for the hill in front of her house to be moved out of her view.

When she got up and saw it still there, she said, "Huh! I didn't think You would do that anyway, God!"

Is that faith? Is that believing God? Yet many Christians today are like that — split personalities..

Getting to that place of total belief and faith in the reality of God is *asking God for a hard thing*. It may take going through some hard places to get there. However, if you sincerely ask, believe me, God will answer.

God Himself asked Abraham, **Is any thing too hard for the Lord?** (Genesis 18:14). Abraham believed God for a hard thing — the birth of a son after he and Sarah were both elderly — and it was counted to him for righteousness. (Romans 4:3.) By the way, he got the son and named him Isaac.

Not long ago, I began to wonder why we were not hearing messages on radio and television about what God is saying in our time, and I asked God what He was saying.

"Nathan," He said, "I am not saying anything."

That scared me, and I asked God what He meant.

He said, "Nathan Simmons, if I walked in the room and sat down on the side of the bed of some of those people who say they know Me and serve Me, it would scare them so badly."

This is an hour when God's people in the majority are not hearing Him.

We are hearing sermons about blessings. We are being entertained. However, we are not really hearing God. It seems we are about at the point for God to step in and show us He is the true and living God, the Alpha and Omega of everything. (Revelation 1:8.)

As we have seen from the history of Israel and Judah, however, for God to get to this point, it may take times of testing. When bad things begin to happen, Christians tend to blame God or doubt Him, or they begin to attribute everything to the devil.

The destruction of Sodom and Gomorrah was of God, yet Lot's wife and daughters acted as if the devil was destroying the sinful cities. (Genesis 19:24-29.) Lot had been praying for a hard thing, for deliverance from the sin in which he and his family lived.

Yet, when deliverance came, he was surprised. His daughters were surprised and took matters of survival into their own hands. His wife grieved over what God was doing, looked back, and became "a pillar of salt" forever. (Genesis 19:26.)

If we are not careful today, we will call what God is doing of the devil, and what the devil is doing of God. We will miss God and become bitter, frustrated, depressed, and aggravated.

If you are going through something that seems bad and troublesome, tell yourself there must be a reason. Seek God to see where hard times are coming from before you begin to rebuke them. Perhaps God is trying to develop character, patience, and strong faith in you.

God: the Same Today, Yesterday, and Forever

God did not just move in the lives of the Israelites. He did not stop carrying out His plan and purpose when Jesus ascended. He did not leave His Church here to flounder along as best we can.

It seems today that the Church is at the place where we can only hold on to what God did in the past. However, that should remind us that what He did once He can, and will, do again. He is the same always. (Hebrews 13:8.) God never changes. (Psalm 15:4.)

We are getting to the place in our nation where God has to do something or darkness will take over. Let me tell you, it is not God who is holding up deliverance. It is us.

Look at all the examples in this book, plus many, many more in the Good Book of how and when God moves on behalf of His people. Always, it is *when they seek Him in repentance.*

> **If my people, which are called by my name, shall humble themselves, and pray, and seek my face, and turn from their wicked ways; then will I hear from heaven, and will forgive their sin, and will heal their land.**
>
> **2 Chronicles 7:14**

We are not living in a time like Jehoshaphat's when the leaders and the people are in the right place with God.

We are not living in a time when it is simple to get God to fight our battles.

We are living in a time when 2 Chronicles 7:14 is a clarion call to the Church.

God did not give the Israelites those words in a time of deep trouble. He spoke those words to Solomon in good times when the Temple was first dedicated.

He meant 2 Chronicles 7:14 to be a promise for all future generations of His people who found bad things happening because they had left God out of their lives and were living wickedly.

He told Solomon what any of His people in future times could do if they had lived in such a way that His judgment was about to fall on them. They could pray, repent, turn from their wicked ways, *and He would heal the land.*

> **If I shut up heaven that there be no rain, or if I command the locusts to devour the land, or if I send pestilence among my people.**
>
> **2 Chronicles 7:13**

Who brings droughts or floods? Who brings insects to eat the crops? Who allows plagues and pestilences? It is God trying to get the attention of, first, His people, and then the unbelievers.

He only brings these things as a last-ditch effort to bring His Church back to the reality of functioning on our knees. They are not the result of His wrath, but His love.

His wrath will not fall on His people, only on the world. (1 Thessalonians 5:9.) Therefore, what we think of as weather disasters, crop disasters, health disasters, are not God's wrath but His trying to get our attention to save us from worse.

One of the final warnings that came to the nation of Israel before they were given over to the Assyrians in captivity and lost their land and freedom was through the prophet Amos. He chastised them for paying tithes and acting religious, but not truly following God.

God, in essence, called them hypocrites and said making sacrifices and keeping rituals was multiplying their transgressions. (Amos 4:4.) It is bad enough to have wicked, hard hearts professing godliness and denying the power thereof, but to appear to be serving God on the outside doubles the sin.

Do we have this going on today? Look at what has happened in our country in the last decade. Does it sound like the cry of God to Israel?

> **And I also have given you cleanness of teeth** (hunger) **in all your cities, and want of bread in all your places:** ***yet have ye not returned unto me,*** **saith the Lord. And also I have . . . caused it to rain upon one city, and caused it not to rain upon another city: . . . So two or three cities wandered unto one** (another) **city, to drink water; but they were not satisfied:** ***yet have ye not returned unto me,*** **saith the Lord.**
>
> **Amos 4:6-8**

God continued to review what He had brought upon the Israelites whose capital was Samaria in an attempt to get their attention: mildew and pests to eat the grapes, the figs, and the olives and the trees thereof. He mentioned pestilences like those that fell on Egypt, and battles in which the young men and horses were killed by the enemy.

If God be for us, who can be against us? However, if we are not for God, then He is not for us, and everyone and everything can be against us.

God spoke to me this way, "Nathan Simmons, anyone who is seeking Me has a sense, an understanding, that I am about to do something that will astound My people as never before."

He will not stop working on us, chastising us, or loving us until we come to the place that we find our greatest pleasure in Him and He can find great pleasure in us.

A recent survey of Christians concluded that "in some ways, we are living in an age of theological anarchy." (See Appendix B.) In other words, a time of transition, which is chaotic, undisciplined, and reflects and attitude of lack of knowledge of God and His Word and a lack of respect for any type of authority.

My concern is where do we go from here? Will we return to God and be like Jehoshaphat and Hezekiah? Or will we be like Israel in the days of Ahab?

Ask God for New Places

I pray that every reader of this book will go to his or her knees and repent if necessary. My prayer is that each one will ask God to move them into new places, not just new levels of where they now are.

Also, I would ask each reader to align himself or herself in the Spirit with all the others praying for the restoration of this nation to God.

There is no space or time in the Spirit. All over the world, God's people need to get in unity and pray first for the Church. Pray for the Church to ask corporately for a hard thing, and that is to be a true witnesses for Jesus.

Then we need to get up off our knees and act in the way that Jesus said would show the world that He was real, that He exists, and that God truly loves the world.

> **A new commandment I give unto you, That ye love one another; as I have loved you, that ye also love one another. By this shall all men know that ye are my disciples, if ye have love one to another.**
>
> **John 13:34,35**

Appendix A

The Saga of Younger Brothers

By the time the descendants of Abraham reached the Promised Land, there were 13 tribes, not just 12, because Joseph's two sons — Ephraim and Manasseh — became counted as the 12th and 13th sons of Jacob and got equal shares. (Genesis 48:5,6,22.)

All the other tribes were called by the names of 11 sons of Jacob. There is no tribe called Joseph. However, there are tribes called Ephraim and Manasseh, the two sons of Joseph.

Genesis 49:3-10 gives us a very interesting account of how Jacob's first three sons forfeited the birthright, and Judah, the fourth son, became the tribe through whom Messiah came. The account is repeated in 1 Chronicles 5:1,2:

> **. . . Reuben the firstborn of Israel** (Jacob), **(for he was the firstborn; but, forasmuch as he defiled his father's bed, his birthright was given unto the sons of Joseph the son of Israel: and the genealogy is not to be reckoned after the birthright. For Judah prevailed above his brethren, and of him came the chief ruler; but the birthright was Joseph's).**

Also, Genesis 48:14-20 tells how Joseph's two sons, Manasseh, the older, and Ephraim, the younger, were switched by Jacob so that Ephraim, the younger, received the birthright blessing of the entire sons of Jacob.

God shows us patterns leading to Messiah through several situations that make pictures, or what the theologians call "typography" showing us Jesus. One of those is what I call "the saga of the younger sons":

1. Adam was God's first "son," the first man created out of matter (Genesis 2:7), and Jesus, the Second Man, the younger, was "the only begotten" Son, who lives to rule and reign with the Father (John 3:16) after Adam defaulted on his responsibilities.

2. Cain, Adam's older son, failed through rebellion and murder, and the younger son, Seth, became the righteous line. (Genesis 4:25,26.)

3. Isaac's older son Esau "despised" his birthright and sold it to Jacob, the younger if only by minutes. (Genesis 25:33,34.) After many testings, Jacob was renamed *Israel* by God and became the third in line of the patriarchs and the founder and father of the Israelites.

4. Other examples include David and Solomon, chosen as the second and third king of Israel over older brothers. (1 Samuel 16:6-13; 1 Kings 2:12.)

Appendix B

Shocking Facts on Born-Again Beliefs[1]

The Barna Research Group, Ltd., an independent marketing research company in California, has been studying cultural trends concerning values, beliefs, attitudes, and behaviors in the United States since 1984.

A recent survey of more than 6,000 randomly selected adults has brought out some insights about beliefs and activities of Christians that the research people called "surprising — and, in some ways, shocking."

More Church of Latter Day Saints (Mormons) said they were born again than either Episcopalians or Roman Catholics! Some 34 percent of Mormons surveyed said they had made a personal commitment to Christ and know they will go to Heaven when they die *only because they have confessed their sins and accepted Jesus Christ as Savior.*

The Protestant denominations with the highest percentage who claimed to be born again are Assemblies of God (81%), other Pentecostal denominations (80%), nondenominational churches (76%), and Baptists (67%).

On the other hand, only 49 percent of the United Methodists interviewed, and only 48 percent of Lutherans, said they were born again.

Some of the other facts revealed by this study are:

- Less than half of all adults in the Christian community believe the Bible is totally accurate.

- Only one-third of them thought they had a personal responsibility to share their faith with others.
- The idea that Satan is a real being is thought by most Americans to be "hogwash." Again, it is surprising that Mormons are most likely to accept Satan's existence at real (59%), while Catholics, Episcopalians, and Methodists are the least likely to do so.
- Seven out of ten think good works can earn salvation.
- Less than half think Jesus lived a sinless life on earth.
- The Barna group found that 12 percent of adults were evangelicals a decade ago, while today only 8 percent are. [They define "evangelical" as someone who believes salvation is only possible as a free gift of God's grace; God is all-knowing, all-powerful, perfect and the Creator; Jesus lived a sinless life on earth; Christians are responsible for sharing the knowledge of Jesus with non-Christians, and Satan is alive and well!]

Barna's comments included the fact that he sees the Christian body in America in the middle of a crisis of biblical illiteracy. He also said that, while many orthodox Christians might disagree with whether that many Mormons are born again, the survey only reflects what the people interviewed believe.

"In many ways," the report says, "we are living in an age of theological anarchy."

Oddly enough, this same survey finds the most common religious practice among Christians is prayer. Bible reading and attending church once a week fell far behind. Also, there is a distinct downward trend in Sunday school attendance.

Another surprise was that most Baptists surveyed had not shared their faith with a nonbeliever in the past year. In the past, Baptists have been generally associated with, or noted for, personal evangelism.

Barna's conclusions are that the data shows "a nation comfortable with religion but not particularly committed to spiritual growth." [The author of this book would call that a clear indication that the Church in the United States has settled down into a "Bethel place" and needs shaking up.]

"Most people describe themselves as religious, describe their faith as being very important in their daily life, but make only a halfhearted effort to truly master the foundations of their chosen faith and live a life determined by that faith," the report concludes.

[Author's Note: The majority of Christians show no signs of wanting to move on to a "Jerusalem place."]

[1]The information from this survey is taken from the following Website:http://www.barna.org/cgibin/PagePressRelease.asp?PressReleaseID=92&Reference=A; also, 93&Reference=A

About the Author

Pastor Nathan L. Simmons is lauded as a powerful man of prayer and the dynamic and anointed leader of a noncompromising Word ministry.

Simmons is a high school graduate who continued his education at a New York City college and graduated from the Manhattan Bible College. It was during this time of preparation that he received and answered the call of God to prayer and consecration.

After giving his life to the Lord at the tender age of sixteen, young Nathan truly committed himself to a ministry of intense prayer, fasting, and consecrated service to God. He transcended this call by further vowing to pray five hours daily and to fast three days weekly. The results of that commitment have been astounding, for Pastor Nathan Simmons has been endowed with a powerful anointing for miracles and deliverance. His radical faith and a burden for the lost have compelled him to offer Christ's message of hope through itinerant evangelism, street witnessing, nursing home, prison and detention center, and homeless shelter ministry – anyplace where broken humanity can be found.

The demand for his anointing has caused Pastor Simmons to traverse the Caribbean, and other places where thousands from all over the world have experienced a unique infusion of power from God through his ministry.

In 1991 Simmons answered the call of God to pastor and established the Citadel of Hope Institutional Church of God in Christ in Atlanta, Georgia. Remaining a fastidious man of prayer, Simmons' Atlanta church has grown to over a thousand and is among the most progressive and fastest growing churches in the area. Hundreds gather on a weekly basis to attend Bible

Exploration, Good Morning Jesus Prayer, and Sunday morning and evening services.

Under the dynamic leadership of this visionary, the Citadel of Hope has impacted the city of Atlanta from its surrounding community to its governing officials. He has received numerous proclamations and commendations from the mayor, the governor, and city council representatives. Prophetically propelled into destiny, this inner-city ministry is multifaceted, community conscious, and innovative in its approach to end-time ministry.